Here's what students of *The Open Mind* are saying:

"What a wonderful place this book has taken me to, where I can become habitual with the breaking of habits, to be coming out of the box I never belonged in, to grow up finally into who I have always been!"
　　　　—Janice, college administrator.

"This has brought me to the awareness that there is no blame. No small thing! There are only a series of journeys and now I know that I have the full capacity inside me to choose to make mine great!"
　　　　—George, counselor of disadvantaged youth

"How do I explain how wonderful it is to be given my true self back from under the heavy lid of definitions and limitations others placed on top of me! I feel as if I'm no longer trying to go home... I have come home at last!"
　　　　—Jan, Stock broker

"I don't believe in angels, but if I did I'd swear one sent me this book. I was ready to quit my job the day I found this by accident in the store. I doled out a chapter at a time over the next ten days, wanting to digest it well. I found myself asking all new questions of myself and others and noticing things I never noticed before. After reading the last chapter, I find myself asking each morning, 'Am I living to the fullest I am capable of?'"
　　　　—Karen, political advisor

"I'm stunned. I don't know exactly what I will do with the things I learned from this book, but I know that I can never again underestimate or undervalue the wisdom that is mine again!"
　　　　—Terri, counselor

"I understand now, after reading this, what I always knew in my heart about my children, but what my mind was afraid to believe—that they, that we all, have unique and discernible gifts that the world needs."
　　　　—Marjorie, parent

"How could any of us stay in a relationship with anyone without knowing the information in this book?"
　　　　—Mason, mediator

"Using these teachings, every single hurtle and point of fear I have had to deal with in working on a film set has been dissolved. I know now how to truly collaborate with others whose minds work differently."

—Etain, actress

"I've found I don't have to try to get through walls anymore, because I know how to find doors."

—Michelle, nurse

"I find myself communicating differently, relating to people differently, understanding myself in new ways. I feel healthier than I ever have before!"

—Cathy, weight loss program instructor

"Knowing these perceptual patterns makes sense of other people without confining or over-simplifying them. It leaves me curious rather than confused or shut down."

—Susan, banker

"I have options now to deal with the issues in my life that I never thought of. I don't always have to verbalize and talk myself into corners."

—Leslie, dancer

"I finally realize that other people understand things in different ways than I do because of the way their minds work. I now know very practical ways to connect with them that I never thought of before."

—George, contractor

"I've learned how to think with my eyes and my hands. I re-learned what I knew as a child—how to have a limber mind."

—Jerry, therapist

"Now I know how to draw passion into my life, how to give it shape and time to form."

—Ivan, business executive

"This approach illuminates a fundamental dimension of human energy which creates understanding, compassion and more effective communication."

—Cindy, zoologist

THE

OPEN
MIND

THE

OPEN

MIND

Exploring the 6 Patterns
of Natural Intelligence

DAWNA MARKOVA, PH.D.

CONARI PRESS
Berkeley, CA

Cover design: Nita Ybarra Design
Cover Illustration:"Rind," copyright © 1996 M.C. Escher/Cordon Art—Baam—Holland. All Rights Reserved.
Author photo: Hollie Noble
Interior Design: Jennifer Brontsema

ISBN: 1-57324-064-8

Library of Congress Cataloging-in-Publication Data
Markova, Dawna, 1942–
 [Art of the possible]
 The open mind : discovering the 6 patterns of natural intelligence / Dawna Markova.
     p.   cm.
 Originally published: Art of the possible. Emeryville, Calif. : Conari Press, 1991.
 Includes bibliographical references and index.
 ISBN 1-57324-064-8 (trade paper)
  1. Thought and thinking.   2. Learning, Psychology of.   3. Interpersonal communication.   I. Title
BF441.M28   1996
153.4—dc20   96-27359

Printed in the United States of America on recycled paper
10 9 8 7 6 5 4 3 2

My grandmother had a small carved walnut box on her bureau.
Inside was a handful of dirt. When I asked her where it came from,
she would only say, "Home." As far as I know, she carried it with her
for over eighty years. When she came to this country, she sprinkled
a pinch of the contents beneath her feet to make a friend of alien ground.

This book contains the seeds that have sprouted in that handful of dirt.
They have waited in the dark, blanketed by various silences and hesitations.
They have been watered with many tears and fertilized by the people
and experiences who were my teachers. I offer them now to your light.

May what came to me as seed be passed on to you as flower.
May it all blossom: the book,
the person writing the book,
the persons reading the book.
May you also pass it on, pass it on to others as fruit.

C O N T E N T S

Chapter 1: Learning is Discovering That Something is Possible, 1

To be educated is not so much to be taught as it is to be awakened to who you really are. **The Open Mind** *invites you to begin the journey of re-naming, re- claiming, un-taming, and re-aiming the dormant capacities of your mind.*

Chapter 2: Becoming Intelligent About Your Intelligences, 15

There are many different kinds of intelligence, many natural aptitudes that combine in unique ways to characterize the thinking pattern of each mind. Here you are offered a tour of the various states of thinking—the way thought is metabolized in the brain to organize, sort, and generate new ideas from your experience.

Chapter 3: The Natural Languages of Your Mind, 33

There are three primary symbolic languages your brain employs to think. Here you discover which one your mind uses to receive and organize information, balance inner and outer experience, and create new patterns from it.

Chapter 4: The True Nature of Our Differences, 63

You are presented with an overview of the six thinking patterns of natural intelligence and several ways of discovering what yours is.

Each of the patterns is presented in depth in the chapters that follow through snapshots, a description of characteristics, a composite portrait, as well as guidelines for getting along with and supporting people whose minds work in this way.

Chapter 5: **AVK**—Auditorily Smart, Visually Centered, Kinesthetically Sensitive, 81

Chapter 6: **AKV**—Auditorily Smart, Kinesthetically Centered, Visually Sensitive, 87

Chapter 7: **VAK**—Visually Smart, Auditorily Centered, Kinesthetically Sensitive, 93

Chapter 8: **VKA**—Visually Smart, Kinesthetically Centered, Auditorily Sensitive, 101

Chapter 9: **KVA**—Kinesthetically Smart, Visually Centered, Auditorily Sensitive, 107

Chapter 10: **KAV**—Kinesthetically Smart, Auditorily Centered, Visually Sensitive, 115

Chapter 11: Coming Home to Yourself, 123

How do you use this information to get unstuck in your thinking, to relate to the "same old problems" in new ways? Through an empirical practice and through stories of how people of each pattern have used this approach, you are offered deeper ways of implementing this information in your life.

Chapter 12: Partnering the Possible—Connecting With Others, 141

How do you use this information in your relationships with others? Here you are offered specific suggestions and practices for communicating with compassion, as well as skills to translate your message into another person's native tongue.

Chapter 13: Living In the Questions, 169

This chapter is a dialogue with some of the questions people ask most frequently as they are learning to understand and integrate this material.

Chapter 14: Risk Your Significance, 187

Here you are invited to explore the larger implications of opening your mind in your life.

Bibliography, 199

List of Charts, 201

Acknowledgments, 203

Index, 205

CHAPTER I

LEARNING IS DISCOVERING THAT SOMETHING IS POSSIBLE

*...and if you know how to look
and learn, then the door is there and
the key is in your hand. Nobody on
earth can give you either that key or
the door to open, except yourself.*

—J. Krishnamurti

To be educated is not so much to be taught as it is to be awakened to who you really are. This chapter invites you to open to the journey.

From My Heart to Yours

The ancient Greeks believed the location of the human mind was in the heart. They reasoned that since the mind was essential, it must inhabit the most vital of all organs. Wounds to the head were not always deadly, but wounds to the heart were. They assumed, therefore, the mind must live in the heart.

If my heart could do my thinking would my brain begin to feel?

—Van Morrison

A friend of mine who is Chinese points to the center of her chest whenever she says, "my mind." She tells me this gesture is common in her culture.

Although we know new blood is constantly flowing through the chambers of our heart, renewing our entire system, once we are adults we assume the capacities of our minds are fixed. We close ourselves off to a myriad of possibilities: "I'm just not an articulate person." Or, "I'm a left-brained kind of a guy." But what if we could open our minds to an inflow of new ideas about what we are capable of doing, knowing and being?

I want to bring you into a comfortable kinship with the open mind of your heart. Hopefully, as a result of reading this book, you will begin to trust yourself and to know the world in new ways. I'd like to think that your curiosity will rekindle into an alive, available resource, and that the barriers you have created—the hard, solid crust that keeps the rest of the world out and you isolated within—will soften into boundaries that define your own space and allow a fundamental intimacy with others.

People Learn in Different Ways

This book invites you to learn how you learn. It will not tell you how smart you are, but it will help you discover **HOW** you are smart. It is written as an operator's manual for adults who are attempting to grow up as they grow older, for adolescents who are about to get their license to drive their minds on their own, for teachers, care givers, and lovers. It is written for anyone who defines himself or herself as a learner, or who has difficulties with recall, organization, or absorption of information and experience. It is for those of us who keep getting stuck in communication gaps when what we are attempting to create is a means of getting through, a meeting place where minds can touch. It is for eagles who are tired of living in cages as if they were chickens.

What is included here is what was excluded from school. The immense educational system in this country teaches people how to do quantum physics (well, some people anyway!), speak German, analyze the syntax of a sentence, and use fancy laboratory equipment and expensive computers, but it never teaches them how to operate their own minds.

We live in an age when we are being forced to deal with rapidly increasing rates of social and political change. The organization of information and the development of human resources is our new frontier. Of necessity, we must learn to facilitate the **process** of learning. Rather than merely accumulating new theories and more information that will be outmoded in a few years, our focus must shift to learning **how** to learn.

You will not find ultimate answers or solutions here, but I hope this book will lead you to a sense of the divine, a respect for the mystery that is involved in being human. It will not tell you where to go or what to do, but it will help you find the path with a gait that is your own. It will not make your life easy, but it will help you understand how you can think, learn, and communicate more effectively.

My intent is to create conditions where you can make discoveries about yourself and others, but there will be no real surprises. The principles are new perspectives of old landscapes, a useful vocabulary which enables you to talk about and grasp what talented communicators, teachers, and therapists have known intuitively all along— that people learn in different ways.

This book will help you understand which of six particular patterns of natural intelligence your mind uses to concentrate, create, and mentate, and to understand its traits, gifts, and idiosyncrasies. This is not a two-dimensional mental technology that you do **to** other people. It is a **guide** for communicating with others at work and home as they are, rather than as you think they should be.

This is not the only model for studying mental syntax, the order

The self is learned. What is learned can be taught.

—Virginia Satir,
Peoplemaking

in which people think. There are systems that utilize similar processes to some you will find in this book, but their more technical emphasis on categorizing the workings of the human mind takes them in a very different direction.

I wrote *The Open Mind* so you could learn to trust your own mind with all of its wild detours and unrelenting obsessions. I designed it so you could rediscover the natural impulses lost from your childhood. I conceived it to help you create confidence in your own capacities.

My hope is that this book will provide you with a frame over which you can stretch the canvas of your own experience. It is meant to give direction and shape, to bring to light the art that lies dormant in your life.

As a heart pumps, it opens and closes. As I've put out these ideas over the last thirty years, there has been a tremendous inflow of feedback from others about how to teach and use them effectively. Consequently, this system itself has continually been transformed.

In rereading the first book I wrote about this approach, *The Art of the Possible,* I realized it did not come near to expressing the collective current thinking about how people's minds work, so I decided to write a new version. What you now hold in your hands is a paper replica of what has been shared with me, a collection of flexing mirrors held up to the light.

The Spring from Which This Book Flows

This approach to understanding how your mind works is based upon a matrix woven together from the wisdom of my grandmother and the most important practitioner and teacher of medical hypnotherapy in this century, Milton Erickson, M.D., as well as research in clinical and educational psychology, perceptual modalities, learning theory, hypnotherapy, expressive arts therapy, and the martial arts. Strands have been added from 30 years of teaching in classrooms, and a private practice in psychotherapy, as well as hundreds of consultations with a broad spectrum of people from business, health care, education and social service organizations.

The coming to consciousness is not a new thing; it is a long and painful return to that which has always been.

—Helen Luke,
The Inner Story

My grandmother taught me that it is possible to see, to hear, to feel through your heart, and that if you really want to understand someone, it's necessary to open your mind. Milton cherished the uniqueness of every human being he came in contact with. Through him, I developed a passionate curiosity about finding each person's unique natural intelligence, and what condition would most help him or her manifest it in the world.

I have been inspired by the excellent and extensive research that Marie Carbo and Kenneth Dunn and others at St. John's University in New York have done into the effects of teaching children to read using their "unique learning style," a combination of perceptual, environmental, and organizational preference.

When I was in graduate school, training in psychological and educational assessment, my professors taught me that we all think in the same way and that some of us have more intelligence than others. But when I was student teaching in the "inner city," the children helped me discover that we are all naturally "abled" in different ways. The ones I was drawn to working with were the "odd ones," those that everyone else had given up on. They were a motley assortment of "unteachables," classified as unsocialized, retarded, learning disabled, autistic, emotionally disturbed, dyslexic, hyperactive—the wounded and broken ones. I was supposed to figure out what was wrong with them, put the diagnosis in black ink on a white form, and keep them out of everyone's way.

I spent three weeks trying to be a "teacher." Control was theirs and my jaws resembled a pair of rusty vise grips. I was thinking seriously of other careers—driving a fork lift truck in Utah, for example. Since there was no way to be Right with these kids, I was terrified. So I did the only thing I knew how to do when terrified: I read a book. Fortunately I stumbled upon one entitled *Beyond Culture*, by an anthropologist named Edward Hall. Although it was neither psychology nor education, the kids I was working with were certainly beyond any culture I had ever known in my sheltered suburban upbringing! While riding the subway from 125th Street to Grand Central Station, the following words by Hall illuminated my desperation:

I do not much believe in education. Each man ought to be his own model, however frightful that may be.

—Albert Einstein

People are different from one another. A leader must be aware of these differences, and use them for optimization of everybody's abilities and inclinations. Management of industry, education, and government operate today under the supposition that all people are alike. People learn in different ways, and at different speeds. Some learn best by reading, some by listening, some by watching pictures, still or moving, some by watching someone do it.... One is born with a natural inclination to learn and be innovative.

—W. Edwards Deming, Ph.D., "A System Of Profound Knowledge"

"All of my experience and research in how people perceive, life experiences teaching various professional groups, clients, students, who image differently in their brains, created sufficient impact to jolt me out of the restraining perceptual and conceptual bonds of my own culture. *I began to ask all students how they remembered things and how their senses were involved in the process of thinking.* Most of them, of course, hadn't the remotest notion of how they thought or remembered and had to go through a long process of self-observation. When they finally did begin to discover something about how their senses were ordered, they invariably jumped to the conclusion that everyone else was just like them, a notion they tenaciously held ... This common projection of one's sensory capacities or lack of them may explain why teachers are frequently impatient with or unsympathetic to students who do not have the same sensory capacities as the teacher."

Not only had I found the information that had been missing in every learning theory I had been taught, but Mr. Hall's words also pointed a finger right to the children. Ask the kids! Why didn't anyone ask the kids how they learned?

I couldn't wait to get to school the next morning, too excited even to do the *New York Times* crossword puzzle on the subway. I burst into the classroom, and before the kids were out of the coat room, I was besieging them with questions about how they learned. Needless to say, my approach was a bit overwhelming. Samantha, who was all pigtails and wide brown eyes, looked at me quizzically and exclaimed, "I don't understand what you are askin' me, Miz Dawna, but you sure got a burnin' in you!"

I humbly spent the rest of the day being dumb, something I had not given myself permission to do since I was five. It became immediately obvious that there were many things these children had already learned how to accomplish. They may have been lost in a world of paper, but there were worlds in which their various intelligences could be found. The standardized IQ tests told me how unsmart they were, but when I was willing to get "dumb," it became obvious **how** they were smart.

Samantha was right. Something in me was burning, and has

continued to for the last 30 years. It takes a lot of hard work to make a young child **not** learn. A lot of control, a lot of de-skilling. When you were young, you learned the incredibly complicated tasks of walking and talking, naturally. You did not have to be motivated or formally instructed. Each of us learns in his or her own time, in his or her own way. An oak already exists inside an acorn; the possibilities of our lives already live within us, waiting for enough warmth and light to unfurl.

It would not be at all accurate to say I discovered the approach that is outlined in this book. Children taught it to me. The Odd Ones. The kids who couldn't, wouldn't, and shouldn't fit into neat little standardized diagnostic compartments. The kids I taught in the slums of Harlem, the migrant labor camp in Coconut Creek, the suburbs of Larchmont, and the back woods of Orfordville. The kids who helped me know that it was **my** responsibility to uncover the specific approach for each of them. It was **my** responsibility to find the needed resource, the ability, the health already there and to foster it. I name them as my teachers, the Joes and Jeromes, the Janes and Samanthas, for they truly have been the muses of this work.

My dream is that one day this book will be passed into some of their hands, whether they are in prison now in Florida, driving a freight train through the corn fields of Iowa, or performing appendectomies in an emergency room in Nairobi. I delight in imagining them reading these words and standing a little straighter as they discover how deep a fingerprint they have left in the wet clay of my mind.

It is, in fact, nothing short of a miracle that the modern methods of instruction have not entirely strangled the holy curiosity of inquiry.

—Albert Einstein

Using This Book

The Open Mind teaches you to use the instrument of your mind to learn more easily and communicate more effectively. There is conceptual information presented for logical, organized understanding; there are narrative descriptions of people applying this approach to their lives, as well as practices for experiential, empirical understanding; there are stories, dreams, and anecdotes to support intuitive comprehension.

In acquiring any new global skill, the initial learning is often a struggle, first with each component skill, then with the smooth integration of components... Later, one almost forgets about having learned to read, learned to drive, learned to draw.

—Betty Edwards,
Drawing on the Right Side of the Brain

When I am teaching, I find myself continually slipping into stories. To know through metaphor is to uncover the design, the pattern of possibilities, the whole of a thing. To know through a story is to know through your heart.

Many of the stories in this book are anecdotes drawn from the lives of people who have studied with me. They are actual, honest-to-goodness people whose stories, statements, and questions are included because their individual journeys seem to transcend personality, and speak in a common voice. Unless labeled so, they are not composites, reasonable facsimiles, or fabrications of my fertile imagination. However, I've disguised names and certain identifying details to protect their privacy, and sometimes presented condensed versions for clarity's sake.

Chapter 2 helps you to identify and understand the functioning of the three different states of consciousness—beta, alpha and theta—that your mind uses to think. Chapter 3 describes the symbolic languages your mind uses to process information in order to organize, sort, and make new patterns from your experience.

Chapter 4 gives you an overview of the thinking patterns as well as some tools to help you discover your own. Chapters 6–10 give you an in-depth understanding of each personal thinking pattern, as well as guidelines for getting along with people whose minds use this form of natural intelligence.

Chapter 11 is concerned with using this skill to meet your personal needs and get unstuck in your thinking, while Chapter 12 concentrates on the application of this skill to relating and communicating compassionately with others. Chapter 13 is an open inquiry, containing the most frequently asked questions about this approach. And Chapter 14 discusses the ethics of using this information and its larger implications.

After making such a fuss over the fact that all minds learn differently, it would be an absurd contradiction to share this model with you in only one way. Therefore, the information of this book is presented using several different processes.

One will ask you to learn through your body, kinesthetically; another will show the information visually, using charts, diagrams, and photographs; still another will present the information through verbal descriptions, dialogues, and interviews. In addition, there are stories and anecdotes to illustrate the specific ways this information can be used in daily situations.

Each will affect you differently. You may find one electrifying, while another may make you yawn so many times your jaw will ache. Please take note of which ones work for you and how you are affected by each. That information is a part of discovering what your mind needs to operate comfortably and effectively.

The data for many of the charts and descriptions was drawn from hundreds of workshops that have been taught all over the country in the past fifteen years. They include traits that have been found to be true in **most** of the people whose minds function in a similar way. In Japan they say a finger pointing to the moon is not the moon. Not every person exhibits every characteristic, and some of us can find characteristics in common with many patterns. These charts are meant as guides; please use them lightly, lovingly, loosely, and of course, with curiosity and compassion.

> Telling ain't teaching and listening ain't learning.
> —Bob Barkley

The Practices

This book invites you to embody your learning through a series of what I call practices. Not exercises. The word exercise is from the Latin word that means "to keep busy." It makes me think of endlessly writing, "I will not throw spitballs at Johnny Marcus" 300 times on a blackboard. It makes me think of doing 125 reps on a Universal machine to strengthen my abdominals. Exercises take us around the same old intersection in the same old way, which is not what is involved in opening your mind.

I decided to use the word "practice" after watching Richard Kuboyama, my Ki-Aikido *sensei* (martial arts teacher), perform an exquisite rolling movement across the padded floor of a gymnasium. I had been attempting to do the same movement for a half hour, but all I had accomplished was a reasonable imitation of a gooney bird trying to get out of its own way. I asked the Sensei how long it had taken him to learn that movement. He replied quietly, "Learned? Oh

I have not learned it yet. I have only been practicing it for 18 years."

My mind began to untwist itself, as it usually did when he spoke, and I asked him how much longer he thought it would be until he learned how to do it. He put one gentle hand on my right shoulder and blinked his brown eyes several times, before replying, "Dawna, I will never **learn** it. I will always just **practice** it. That's all there really is in life, you know. Just practice."

A real story touches not only the mind, but also the imagination and the unconscious depths in a person, and it may remain with him or her acquiring any new global skill, the initial learning is often a struggle, first with each component skill, then with the smooth integration of components... Later, one almost forgets about having through many years, coming to the surface of consciousness now and then to yield new insights.

—Helen Luke,
The Inner Story

This book contains many practices. They are designed to help you inhabit what you are learning, to make you an active participant in this process instead of a passive receptacle to whom teaching is done. Doing is part of knowing. The practices included here will become a bridge between your intellect and your intuition.

Most of them are designed so that you can read each step and then go inside and do the work in your mind. A few will necessitate having someone else read them to you as you do them or reading them to yourself on a tape recorder and listening to your own voice guide you. Most of them contain seed questions that will germinate as you reflect on your own experience.

Many of them have been originated by me. Others have been learned during workshops and seminar experiences in which I have participated as a student. Trying to give credit to their originator would go something like this: "I learned this in a workshop with Jean who learned it from Ilana who got it from Fritz, who..." I've attempted to attribute as accurately as I could, but I'm sure I've omitted many sources. This is not in any way due to any lack of respect or appreciation for my teachers.

Fostering a Beginner's Mind

In using this book, please feel free to find which form of learning works for you and follow that. You may want only linear information, and find everything else "beside the fact." It is. Follow your inclination. Perhaps that will give your mind the safety it needs to go back later and adventure through the empirical learnings or even meander in the metaphors.

What is essential is that you take responsibility for your own learning. Trust your way. Befriend your mind, give it what it needs. It takes all your courage to be the person that you are, to fulfill your odd and unique possibilities. **How** you use this book will teach you more about the workings of your mind than its contents ever could. Start by making a mistake on purpose, flagrantly. Any mistake will do. Drop the book on your foot. Squeeze the toothpaste from the middle of the tube. Spell a word the wrong way on purpose.

Schools teach us to groove in our mistakes. We are taught they are the equivalent of being "wrong." How many did you get "wrong" on your spelling test? By the time we are adults, our conscious minds follow suit, proving our schools are right, even if what they are right about is how wrong we are.

If left untutored, the human brain will **discard** mistakes and groove in successes. A baby learning to suck its thumb does not keep putting that thumb in its ear. One time in the ear, another in the nose, maybe even a third in the eye. But once that thumb reaches that mouth, within minutes you have a lovely, natural, neurological groove.

Unfortunately, we are too often taught to act sophisticated, to stay the same, while pretending to be wise. We hang on to our habitual, known ways of being at least as hard as they hang on to us. That's because one of the worst things to be in this culture is a beginner. The word conjures up feelings of awkwardness, sweaty palms, a throat that needs to be cleared again and again. Yet in the Orient, a beginner is honored for her curiosity, respected for his vitality, welcomed for the freshness he or she may bring. Beginners make sure that ideas maintain flexibility rather than "rigidify" into dangerous dogma.

I remember reading an interview with Wanda Landowska, the world's greatest harpsichordist. Everyone was shocked to learn that at age 75, she had begun to take classes again as a beginner! When asked why, she was reported to have rolled her eyes back in her head, as she declared, "Oh my yes, the delights and joys of being a beginner again! The freshness, the vitality of experiencing it all for the first time…"

I am inviting you to risk thinking like Wanda. Become a begin-

> That so few dare to be eccentric marks the chief danger of the time.
> —John Stuart Mill

ner again in knowing the instrument of your mind. Roam around in the untrampled grass for a while rather than trudging through the known pathways you have been using for years. You may get lost, you may stir up a swarm of mosquitoes, you may not recognize where you are going, but you may also find yourself touching a very clear space, a self that you knew quite well long, long ago.

There should be less talk. A preaching point is not a meeting point.

—Mother Theresa

Practice:
Honoring Your Wisdom, Finding Your Intent

1. Think of a time in your life when you learned something well **and** enjoyed yourself in the process. Do a slow motion instant replay in your mind as many times as you need to until you become aware of specifically how you learned to do it. (For example, "I felt my body begin to do it, then I saw a Technicolor movie in my mind, filling up my whole head, and then I told myself to begin.")

2. Think of a time in your life when something was very difficult for you to learn and very frustrating. Review it as you did above to discover specifically how the process was different.

3. How do you know when you learn something? Again, please be as specific as you can. (For example, "I know because I can tell someone else," or "I can feel it in my solar plexus," or ...)

4. Please make your intent explicit: that is, write down, or put on a tape recorder, or tell someone, or go for a walk and feel *what it is that you want to learn as a result of reading this book.*

You Are Not Unique in the Same Way as Everyone Else

Education is meant to help you realize your individuality. It should bring to maturity the talent that already waits dormant within you, invisible, inaudible, untouched.

You and I are now responsible for our own education—it is never too late to learn. Coming to know your personal thinking pattern and how to use it is like coming to discover how to use a bow to play a violin. Please remember, however, as you find your pattern in the pages that follow, that these are not concrete compartments or definitions of who you are. There are cultural and gender variations within each one. All people with red hair do not really have the same hair color. Any two violins have variations in the sound that is produced by them. It is my hope that the material you find here will support your thinking of your mind as a door, no, a thousand doors opening past the limitations of your previous history, so you become more and more like who you really are, closer and closer to your true natural intelligence.

> The question is not whether we will die, but how we will live.
>
> —Joan Borysenko, Ph.D,
> *Guilt Is the Teacher,*
> *Love is the Lesson*

BECOMING INTELLIGENT ABOUT YOUR INTELLIGENCE

An open mind is all very well,
but it ought not to be so open that
there is no keeping anything in or out
of it. It should be capable of shutting
its doors sometimes or it may be
found a little drafty.
—Samuel Butler

There are many different kinds of intelligence, many natural aptitudes that combine in unique ways to characterize the thinking pattern of each mind. What we will uncover in this chapter—the various states of thinking, the way thought is metabolized in the brain to organize, sort, and generate new ideas from your experience—is the first step to becoming intelligent about your different intelligences.

This morning, while waiting behind a red van at the local gas station, no matter what else I tried to pay attention to, all I could hear was a conversation between the woman passenger, who was leaning out of the window, and her husband, a hunched-over man who was filling the tank. The metallic tone of her voice vibrated in my skull. "How could you think like that? What's wrong with you? Are you crazy or lazy or what? Talk to me, Herman! Don't give me one of those silent treatments again, Herman, talk to me!"

As annoying as she was at 7 A.M., this woman was operating from one of the most common misconceptions of our culture—the assumption that her husband's mind should work just like hers and that, as a matter of fact, all minds should work in the same way. When the evidence is otherwise, as it was with Herman, we make "other" wrong—stupid, slow, crazy, incompetent, disorganized, disabled, stubborn, shy, or plain old weird.

The assumption that all of us use our brains in the same way to think has led to mis-appraisal of our core competencies, as well as to ruptured relationships. When some of us learn easily and others don't, we've been told that the reason is some people are smart and others not, some are creative, articulate, logical and others not. Too many of us have been exiled from our native truth because we have not been taught to listen or speak in its tongue.

In truth, our minds are like the instruments of an orchestra. Imagine what it would be like if we assumed that music could only be played on one instrument. In reality, there are many different instruments that can each play music differently. This approach to the different patterns of natural intelligence separates out the stringed instruments from the woodwinds, the harmonicas from the kettledrums. One does not play them in the same way. Knowing the kind of instrument you have helps you know whether to put it to your lips or use a bow. Remember, though, that each violin, each kettledrum, each flute has its own sound. The six personal thinking patterns offered in this book are meant to help you discover the type of instrument your mind uses, so you can play the music you want with it in the way it was designed to be played.   .

95% of what we know about how we think, that is virtually all of the current information about the chemical, physiological and psychological functions of the brain, has emerged in the last 10–15 years.

—Henriette Ann Klauser, *Writing on Both Sides of the Brain*

The specific gifts of each instrument are revealed, the harmonics that are possible between us become apparent once we understand and honor the unique ways our minds function. Each of us has a particular pattern—a natural intelligence—our own way of taking information in, storing it, generating and expressing it. To know how to access the specific pattern your mind utilizes can be as useful as knowing your PIN number for the automatic bank teller or having the key to your safe deposit box. How can you spend all of the resources you really have if you don't know how to retrieve them?

The woman in the red van is not alone. I've come to realize that many misunderstandings, fights, and learning and communication problems are caused by not knowing the pattern a particular mind uses to think. When something works properly, we assume it was due to some magical external force, like luck. When it fails, it never occurs to us that we might simply be using the wrong technique: trying to blow on a violin or pluck a flute. We just think we have to blow faster, to pluck harder.

I'd like to introduce you to some people who came to me with common problems that were a result of just such misunderstandings and lack of information.

Sally is beside herself with frustration. She crosses and re-crosses her white-stockinged legs, then fluffs her newly permed brown hair. She touches an immaculate handkerchief to her nose. Her seven-year-old son, Richard, is running haphazardly around the room, throwing a Nerf basketball into a plastic hoop mounted on the door. Her eyes dart to follow him, wary, waiting. Her voice is nasal, almost whining, and the rhythm of her words is as rapid as that of Richard's red high-top sneakers.

"I have to tell you, he's been tested and the school psychologist insists he is hyperactive and oppositional. They demand I put him on medication. He just will not behave. I am so frustrated I don't know what else to do. I've read some studies in my nursing journal that say there are possible side-effects to the drug, but the school wouldn't recommend anything that would hurt him, would they?

"He has to learn to pay attention. When I try to talk to him, engage him in almost any conversation, he just goes deaf and dumb.

Our mind creates categories—space and time, above and below, inside and outside, myself and others, cause and effect, birth and death, one and many—and puts all physical and psychological phenomena into categories like these before examining them and trying to find their true nature. It is like filling many different shapes and sizes of bottles with water in order to find out the shape and size of water.

—Thich Nhat Hanh,
The Sun My Heart

I give up! Last week I took him for a walk in the woods and he was actually violent. He picked up a stick and started hitting a beautiful poplar tree.

"His father and I have joint custody, but I don't talk to his father. He drives a trailer truck. I believe that unless we attend to this immediately, Richard will grow up to be… just like him!"

• • •

We live in a time of Great Social Crisis. Our children rank at the bottom of nineteen industrial nations in reading, writing, and arithmetic.

—John Gatto, New York City Teacher of the Year

Jim and Susan have been working with several different therapists for the past two years. They have each been married before and live with three children. People describe them as an ideal couple, but they have begun to discuss divorce. He is a computer genius, who dresses for comfort only, and has lines of despair etched into his face. Susan, though fashionably attired, drags herself around like a creature who has gnawed off its own legs. Her eyes reflect the sad, broken kind of beauty that one reads about in gothic novels.

"She's frigid. I know that's not the kind of thing I'm supposed to just lay out, but it's true. Obviously she doesn't feel any passion for me anymore. She's an ice cube. She never wants to **do** anything. We used to go camping together a lot. But now she's too tired. Every night when I come home from work, she's got a list of things for me to do. No hugs, no affection. I'd give anything for her just to grab me or rub my feet. It doesn't have to be sex all the time, but that wouldn't be bad once in a while too, ya know? I just need some warmth."

"He's the one who's not attracted to me. Look at him—it's written all over his face. He falls asleep in front of the TV every night. The romance is over. I guess we're incompatible or something. I've tried to give him a massage, but he just gets sexual immediately. Maybe I don't feel anything for him anymore. I don't know what I feel. I just don't see any way out. It's the same blind alley no matter where I look!

• • •

Matt is a high-school baseball coach as well as the shop teacher. Most of the kids who are in some kind of trouble come to him to get advice or just talk things over. He is a tall and attractive man who moves as if he has ball bearings built into the soles of his feet. He's been talking for years about going to graduate school to become a guidance counselor, but that's all it's ever been—talk.

"People have been telling me for so long to take the entrance exams and go back to school, but they don't understand . . . I can't take the written tests, I freeze up somehow and my mind goes blank. Then I panic. How could I go to graduate school, if I can't take a test or write a paper? Ask me what I know and I'll talk your ear off, but when I have to write it down I just space it out. It's like I steal things with my eyes, and then lose what I've just stolen. I'm bored with teaching shop, but it's probably what I'll be doing for the rest of my life, because I can't make it in a paper world."

• • •

Joyce is a first-year medical student who earned a Ph.D. with honors in biology. Raised by a desperately poor farm family in South Carolina, she carries all of their hopes for the future on her shoulders. She is a wiry woman, connected to her body in the same way a city is connected to its electrical energy supply. She hesitates, stammers intermittently, stumbles with her words, eyes searching the corners of the room as if looking for a spider to examine.

"I don't get it. I worked hard, but college and grad school were a snap for me. I've always loved lab sciences, always done real well too. I decided to become a doctor so I could make my parents proud of me. I'm the only person in the family to even make it through high school. I want to give something back to my people. I feel like I'm **meant** to be a doctor. Maybe I'm a little too sensitive now and then, but I care a lot, deep down in me. I feel for people in pain and I want to help them. I never expected to have trouble in medical school. I don't know what's wrong with me. I sit in those big lecture classes and just space out. I get numb or something. We have small discussion seminars afterwards and I freeze up, I can't say a word. Nothing comes out. I want to die, I mean really. I'm gonna flunk out if this goes on much longer. The dean called me in and said he isn't sure I have what it takes. I'm not sure I do either. I feel like killing myself a lot lately. It's not easy being a black woman in medical school you know, and I just can't seem to hack it."

• • •

In the coming world, they will not ask me, "Why were you not Moses?" They will ask me, "Why were you not Zusya?"

—Zusya

Each of these people thought there was something wrong with them. Each of them came to me expecting to have what was wrong with them treated, fixed, changed. Sometimes I think it is fortunate that medical science can't yet do brain transplants, since in this age of Disposable Everything, most of these people would have traded in their original equipment for new left frontal lobes!

Instead I taught them how to use the equipment they had in the way it was designed to work. Each of their brains took experience in, and translated it into a unique pattern; the difficulties they were recounting were mainly the result of not understanding how to use their minds effectively. We'll return to these people shortly, but first let's turn to you and the way thought is digested in your brain.

Never try to teach a pig how to sing. It wastes your time and annoys the pig.

—Source unknown

Mental Metabolism

Contrary to what Mrs. Chalkdust may have tried her best to get it to do, your mind, any human mind for that matter, does not stay still; instead it flows in and out of different states of consciousness, following its own tides and rhythms. If you've ever tried to "pay attention" to any one thing for an extended period of time (doing your income taxes, for instance, or driving late at night on a highway), you've already noticed that your thoughts will not always march in step to your command.

As I begin writing this page, for example, my attention fades in and out like a short-wave radio. Drifting, I become aware of my left ankle rubbing against my right heel. I smell the cedar chips newly spread in the garden. Then I feel clouds in my mind and I lose awareness of the moment. I'm thinking about… I'm not sure what I'm thinking about or even if I'm thinking. Now I am hearing the keys of my computer clicking and the telephone ringing in the kitchen downstairs. The small black letters come into focus as they spill across the screen. My thoughts are clear, alert, attentive again.

My mind has evidently decided to begin teaching you about this system by demonstrating the different states of consciousness as my fingers dance across the gray plastic keys to write about them. If I had been hooked up to an electroencephalogram (EEG machine), it would probably have shown my brain waves changing from mostly beta waves to a preponderance of alpha waves to primarily theta waves and then back again as I changed ways of thinking from focused to receptive to entranced to focused again. Most people just refer to these three as paying attention, mind wandering, and "spacing out."

As far as we know now, the waking mind operates on three levels, or thinking states: what is commonly called conscious, subconscious, and unconscious. To make the flow of thought through these states visible, we'll follow the logic of a spiral. (See diagram on page 22.)

Starting at the center point, you are conscious of a thought, attentive, focused, concentrating, linear and detail-oriented. Your brain is producing mostly beta waves.

As you relax, as the thought begins to become digested, sorted out, your attention becomes more diffuse; the spiral opens into what we are calling the subconscious level. This is where you might experience yourself as confused or wondering or perplexed. Your brain generates more alpha waves here.

As the thought becomes integrated, filed, stored, made into new patterns in the unconscious level, your attention becomes the most diffuse of all. The spiral is now fully open, wide, expanded, and you are "lost in thought." In this cradle of your innermost awareness, your brain is generating more theta waves.

Like a beam of a flashlight, your attention covers a wider area of possibilities, becoming more and more diffuse as you open your mind to expand your consciousness. You grow more and more receptive in order to access the most innovative and generative theta aspects of your brainpower.

To summarize, as thought moves wider and wider in the spiral, it becomes more and more symbolic, receptive, intuitive, sensitive, private and intimate. And we are less and less aware of it, less able to concentrate on one thing. If you communicate from the widest place in the spiral, what comes out may be inspired, and rich in imagery, but it may also be confusing to others or seem very circular and abstract, lacking the details that make it coherent.

As a number of scientists have noted, research on the human brain is complicated by the fact that the brain is struggling to understand itself.... The existence in every brain of two different cognitive modes is no longer controversial since the work of Roger Sperry.... Studies at Cal Tech indicate that each mode of thinking, each hemisphere, receives reality in a different way.... Scientists are still struggling with where the different modes of thinking actually are located in the human brain and how the organization of these modes vary from individual to individual.

—Betty Edwards,
*Drawing on the Right Side
of the Brain*

To transform the world we must begin with ourselves; and what is important in beginning with ourselves is the intention. The intention must be to understand ourselves and not to leave it to others to transform themselves...

—J. Krishnamurti,
The First and Last Freedom

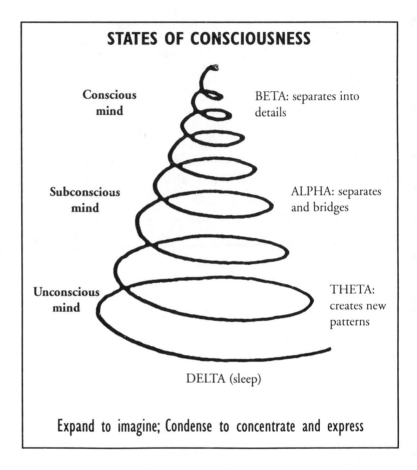

STATES OF CONSCIOUSNESS

Conscious mind

BETA: separates into details

Subconscious mind

ALPHA: separates and bridges

Unconscious mind

THETA: creates new patterns

DELTA (sleep)

Expand to imagine; Condense to concentrate and express

When you wish to attend to linear tasks, to concentrate on one thing (such as balancing your checkbook) or make a decision, you condense your attention down through the alpha state—the bridge between your inner and outer worlds—to the (beta) laser beam point of greatest focus, the conscious "point," of your mind. Here it is most easily expressed. Here it can be readily retrieved or recalled. Here, we tend to be more confident, but also more critical and linear.

Expanding, contracting, expanding, contracting, your mind moves like your lungs or heart; widening as it opens to digest and create new patterns in your unconscious mind, contracting as it concentrates to express them through your conscious mind.

Getting Wet

One of Milton Erickson's favorite expressions was, "You can't learn to swim on a piano bench." As we proceed in this exploration of the different functions of these states of mind, it's now time to get wet—to dip in your toes and experience each one. In this way, you will have a personal reference point and cellular comprehension of the water we'll be swimming in.

There is a time for expansion and a time for contraction; one provokes the other and the other calls for the return of the first.

—Swami Vivekananda

The Many Ways of Knowing:
The Conscious State

Begin by getting yourself to "pay attention" in the way that is most usual for you. Notice exactly what you need to do. Some people open their eyes wider looking at every detail, some sit up straighter, changing their physical posture, some listen more attentively. You probably have your own set of adjustments that are automatic. Please put the book down and bring your awareness to what is most helpful for you to do so you can pay attention in this way.

You've just experienced the state of mind that most people use to think in a linear, logical, rational, "reasonable" or, as some people refer to it, left-brained way. I call it the "one-way mind," because in this state, we tend to be certain there is only one way to think about something, and we like to get right to the point. This is where we are most comfortable and competent receiving information and expressing ourselves in public, and where we are the least distractible.

When the brain produces mostly beta waves, we are most alert and least receptive. We say we "remember." This state of mind is the home of the tried and true, because it loves grooves, routines, rules, details, and orderly things that behave as expected. Its purpose is separation and discrimination. Thus everything becomes partitioned into objectified units.

This is where patterns are memorized; once familiar, these are used to make decisions in unfamiliar situations. If you come upon an unknown object in the road, hear a strange sound in the night, or smell something unrecognizable, your mind will use the conscious mode to identify what it is and why it is there. This is what prevents you from sticking your hand in the fire over and over and makes it possible not to need to experiment with each new danger before avoiding it.

Possibilities are eliminated here. The word "decide" comes from the same root as homicide or suicide, and it means to cut off or kill off all possibilities except one. For example, if I hear a sound in the night that is unfamiliar, not the way I think things should sound, I get very alert, and my conscious mind does its job of separating out that sound from every other one in the house until I can identify it: "Ah yes, that's the new refrigerator making ice cubes." If you couldn't think in this mode, your world would become a chaotic whirlpool.

We have been taught that if we aren't in this state, we aren't learning. In fact, this is only the very first stage in the process. Here we accumulate information for the short term, but don't necessarily "learn" it. I once studied fiercely for a geology exam and got an "A." The next day, walking through Central Park, a friend asked me whether a particular boulder was igneous or metamorphic and I didn't have the slightest idea. The information had gone in one eye and out the other.

The conscious mind is like the mouth of the mind that takes information in and chews it up, but doesn't swallow or digest it. If you think of your whole mind as a library of information, then the conscious mode would be the card catalog. It can help you find a book and information about it, but you still have to get it from the stacks and read it in order to be informed by what it has to offer. The beta mind likes and needs order and responds well to structured activities.

It is here that you are most actively engaged with the outside world. You are intentional, goal-oriented, productive. The Eighties were a decade of this state of consciousness, since this kind of precise, quick thinking is what is needed for competition and getting ahead. My father was my primary teacher of this state, pushing me to struggle to "climb the ladder of success. It's a dog-eat-dog world. You've got to fight to get ahead." This is the marketplace mentality.

There is another side to this way of thinking. For one thing, it

> Education consists mainly in what we have unlearned.
>
> —Mark Twain

does not deal well with change. The conscious mind loves stability and will do whatever is necessary on the surface to achieve it. In a relationship, a person making change from this place would go for the kiss-and-make-up technique, while an organization would go for the quick fix. Because of its obsession with familiar patterns and repetition of the known, and its difficulty rejecting them once established, the conscious mind plays a large part in addiction, which is progressive and repeated familiar behavior.

Most of our beliefs and self-concepts reside here and can become rigid, calcified dogma. It is the most difficult part of your mind to change. Have you ever met someone who is beautiful or brilliant but believes herself to be a mediocre slob? Have you ever tried to change her mind? Like a dictator, the conscious mind wants to control everything. It becomes very involved with the meaning of things, and with proving it is RIGHT! Its favorite vocabulary is, "I think," "I've decided," "I know," "In my opinion," "What I mean is..."

Thus, concentrating in a focused and alert way is very useful for figuring out your income taxes, fixing something that's broken, or for getting raises and promotions. But opening your mind into alpha and theta thinking is most effective when you want to create, or relate, heal, or understand the whole of a system.

> It is better to give and receive.
>
> —Bernard Gunther

The Many Ways of Knowing: The Subconscious State

Let's shift states of mind and go a little wider. Think of a time when you split your awareness, thinking about one side of an issue and then the other, going back and forth between two options. "On the one hand... but on the other..." To do this, you'll have to get confused or perplexed and space out a little. Let your thinking get a little fuzzy, as if you can't make up your mind about something. Perhaps you begin to muse or daydream, and your mind wanders. You may feel as if you are present and yet gone, as if your consciousness is internal and external at the same time.

As you bring that experience to mind, notice what you need to do to think in this state. Some people, for example, need to stare or focus their eyes, some need to begin to hum in their minds or say certain words over and over. Other people need to just notice their breath and let their body relax. What's your particular way? How do you shift into this way of thinking? Notice what this state of consciousness is like for you.

… in the plant there is a layer—sometimes only one cell wide—between the tissue of the root and the shoot. It is a crossing point between earth and sun… The two realms are an organic breathing continuum.

—M.C. Richards,
The Crossing Point

This too **is** thinking, no matter what Mr. Straightnarrow told you in fifth grade. In fact, when you allow yourself to be comfortably perplexed, you may discover your "confusion" has changed altogether and become curiosity.

In this binary age, the trend is to describe humans as having two modes of thinking: rational ("left brain") and imaginative ("right brain"). However, my doctoral studies of hypnotherapy, as well as recent research in meditation and the martial arts, indicate there is a third mode. You might think of it as shifting into a neutral gear, to pause and sort out what is self and what is other, what will be kept and what will be discarded.

When the brain is producing the most alpha waves, that is our in-between state, the revolving door of our minds where the vast array of input we receive from the outer world is sorted. It is a transitional (trance-itional) way of thinking, for here the brain is metabolizing information and exploring options. It is a state of mind that is engaged by experimentation and resists too much external structure. It is thinking in dualities, a two-way mode: "Either I do this or that; either his side of the story is wrong or hers is wrong; either I see it this way or that."

It is like the stomach of the mind, churning things around, deciding what will be digested and how. In the case of the new refrigerator, I might listen to it for a while and figure out whether I want to go on listening to that noise or get up and close my bedroom door. Because it links the conscious and unconscious mind, this transitional way of thinking can perceive the details of something and the whole of it.

In fact, this way of thinking is vital for decision-making and image making, for it is the bridge between our inner and outer worlds. Without it, we'd swallow everything whole, never thinking about whether something is right for us or not. Knowing this makes it easier to expand when we're "confused," giving our brains the time they need to cross that bridge comfortably. The subconscious functions as a threshold where our inspiration and wisdom are distilled before being expressed. It is a domain that is **both** public **and** private, receptive and active, between our interior and exterior minds, where we are motivated into action and soothed into relaxation.

Here the strange becomes familiar and the familiar becomes strange. Here your system is trying to integrate, take stock, screen, filter, pause, and catch up. It is attempting to help you discover what **you** think, as it balances your needs and those of others. This is what determines whether you are overwhelmed or in charge.

My mother was my primary teacher of the subconscious mind. She was always weighing both sides of any decision, terrified to act lest she make a mistake: "Well, you could wear the red dress, but it's a little flashy. On the other hand, you could wear the blue one, but it's too casual." Since most of us are taught in school that this way of thinking means we don't know what we're supposed to, we develop the habit, as my mother did, of contracting ourselves here, getting "up-tight" and uncomfortable when we hang out in this mode for any length of time. When people feel pressured, they are usually stuck here, thinking they need to return to the conscious mind immediately.

Change from this state is actually effected by taking time to step back and reflect, by not deciding until the information is sorted and completely digested, by taking a "wait-and-see" attitude. Giving ourselves time to be here, to wait and not know, is crucial to healing, and often uncomfortable until we get used to it.

Although this way of thinking may not seem to produce the most meaningful ideas or action, a person's whole life revolves around this passageway. Some common vocabulary from this mode is, "Um...," "Wait a minute...," "No thanks," "I'm not ready to decide that now." "It seems to me you are **both** right," "I pass." "I need some space."

> The soul should always stand ajar. Ready to welcome the ecstatic experience.
>
> —Emily Dickinson

The Many Ways of Knowing: The Unconscious State

*To explore theta thinking, allow yourself to remember a time you really spaced out and were lost in your thoughts. Perhaps driving on a highway at night when you were at exit 15, then suddenly you noticed you are at exit 19? What happened to exits 16, 17 and 18? Who **was** that masked person driving your car?*

This is a time of taking a brief (or extended) mental vacation. Your thoughts go wide and receptive, or for some people very deep. There's no need here to control anything, to be anything, to do anything or know anything. This is a very private and often peaceful way of knowing. Some people describe this as floating. Some close their eyes. Others just listen to the stillness or rock back and forth. What is your unique way of entering this state of mind? Put the book down after reading this paragraph and just allow your mind to wander wherever it wants to go for a few moments, as it does when you're listening to a boring lecture or waiting alone in a movie theater for the show to begin.

After you have rested here for a few moments, notice what you need to do to focus your attention and bring yourself to the present moment again?

We remember wholeness so readily, because we don't have very far to look for it. It is always within us, usually as a vague feeling or memory left over from when we were children. But it is a deeply familiar memory, one you recognize immediately as soon as you feel it again, like coming home after being away a long time. When you are immersed in doing without being centered, it feels like being away from home. And when you re-connect with being, even for a few moments, you know it immediately. You feel like you are at home no matter where you are and what problems you face.

—Jon Kabbat-Zinn, Ph.D., *Full Catastrophe Living*

The state of mind you just experienced, where the brain is producing mostly theta waves, is often referred to as right–brained, spaced out, or meditational. The unconscious mind (which I really think should be re-named something grand, like the Transconscious) is no more apparent in daily life than the growth of a tree in the midst of an opaque winter day. This mode may not seem ordinarily "awake," but it is very much alive, functioning as source and guide just as the heartwood of that tree is.

Schools strengthen linear, beta thought at the expense of intuition and inspiration. Our culture rewards verbal over non-verbal thinking. Thus we have been taught to distrust, be superstitious about, be afraid of, and consider irrelevant our source and guide, the unconscious mind. In order to reclaim it, we must relinquish our belief that the linear is superior or more worthy. The bark is no more worthy than the heartwood.

This expansive state of mind, where curiosity becomes wonder, awe, or surprise, is often the most difficult for us to access and, for many people, where they feel the most shy, awkward, or vulnerable. That's because we have been taught that to think this way is to waste time. In our culture, we are supposed to be in action or reaction as much as possible. No one gets good grades or promotions for thinking in this way. If someone is busy "doing" something, we are taught not to interrupt. But in the east, where reflection is honored, no one would interrupt someone who was sitting quietly in contemplation!

You probably learned to apologize for thinking this way in school, for "daydreaming," and not paying attention to the teacher. In fact, in this state, your brain was processing what you were learning, searching internally for how the new information fit with what you already had experienced, making new patterns from it, storing information for the long term, and dreaming new possibilities for the future. Here you think about the way things could be.

In theta, the brain thinks in many ways at once, as if in a web, creating and carrying messages indirectly through dreams, symbols, and imagery. Because it can think in so many directions simultaneously, this mode enables us to be alive in the contradictions that challenges offer. It searches for the pattern that will reveal the whole of something, the forest rather than the trees. In the now-famous case of the refrigerator, the unconscious mind might incorporate the sound into the whole of a night by giving one a dream about being in a hailstorm.

I think of this most receptive state as the tomb, the loom, and the womb, since all of our life experiences are stored here, constantly being woven into ever-changing patterns with our new experiences, and seeding our creativity with unlimited dreams of possibilities. Because it is the mode of thought most capable of understanding the whole of something, the big picture, the widest landscape, this is also the place of deepest spiritual connection and healing, of that elusive inner voice or insight or gut feeling.

Metaphorically speaking (which is what makes the most sense in this way of thinking), your unconscious mind is the navigator, the stacks of the library, the floor of the ocean where all your life experi-

> It doesn't matter who my father was; it matters who I remember he was.
>
> —Anne Sexton

Every child is an artist. The problem is how to remain an artist once she grows up.

—Pablo Picasso

ences drift down, are stored, and change form. If the conscious mode is the one with which you are powerful by actively extending influence, the unconscious is the one with which you are powerful by **being** influenced. The former perceives the details: "That tree is a Casurina pine." The latter perceives the whole: "I am enveloped in a forest of rustling green, sticky sweet sap…" The beta mode separates and ranks, the theta connects and links. The unconscious mind wants free play, no external structure, self-direction.

It is from this private, inner-directed consciousness you join with and become Michael Jordan when he leaps, the violin in a Mozart sonata, Aunt Agatha when she weeps. It is also the home of your least accessible, least controllable, least discernible self, who is always working on your own behalf.

Theta thinking is continually seeking, searching, wondering, experimenting. It is concerned with function and approach rather than meaning; it cares about process, not product. It is also the place needs spring from, including your need to be looked at, listened to, and touched. Solving problems is irrelevant to this mode, yet it can discern the pattern in the problem in fresh and new ways, always finding the possibility for connection.

This is not the way they think in the military. When put behind a weapon, this mind automatically becomes the target: "I know I'm supposed to shoot this guy, but he's so young. He probably has kids at home just like mine. And a wife with brown hair like Alice's." It makes associations by connecting something in the present to an experience in your history: "The sound of that firecracker reminds me of the mortars I heard in Vietnam." It is the healing, compassionate, empathic mind of your heart: "Make love not war"; "Become one with the universe."

My grandmother, who delivered hundreds of babies into the world and sat with an equal number of people as they died and left the world, was my teacher of this mind. She taught me indirectly, through stories, symbolic rituals and ceremonies, how things were interrelated.

This mode of thinking is devoted to understanding how things are connected. It functions very much like a kaleidoscope, recombining bits and pieces to make new images and symbols. I think of Thomas Edison, who found a solvent for rubber by putting bits of it into every solution he could find, while all the other scientists were approaching the problem theoretically.

To your unconscious mind, change is *of* the system, not just *to* it. When change comes from this place, you become a non-smoker rather than switch brands. You go into therapy to study the process of how you are or are not relating to your spouse. Your business decides to do an overview of how information is moving throughout the company, rather than to fire the computer operator. The government does an in-depth overhaul of its financial system instead of starting a new lottery.

However, this mode of thinking cannot make boundaries, differentiate, or discriminate. It is a wild jungle, mystical and inventive. "What about this way—but maybe if we did it like this…" It is never satisfied, because it has no specific destination. Westward ho to anyplace!

This is where we get lost when we "lose touch with reality." It is also where we go to experience transcendent phenomena. It is how we, as humans, can take leftover loss and joy and spin them into sonnets and sonatas.

The vocabulary of this state of consciousness is one of wonder and association: "I wonder what would happen if we made sidewalks move…" "This meeting is like leftover chopped liver!" "You're just like my Uncle George, that nasty man!"

Since there is no way for it to be wrong or right, the creative mind can join with any one else's perspective, "Oh, I see what you mean." "Of course now that you put it that way…" "That sounds like a possibility." This way of thinking can result in the loss of a sense of self, in deception, and an inability to separate fantasy from reality. It can also result in an Albert Schweitzer, a Mother Theresa, and a Thomas Edison.

In summary, each mode of thinking has its burdens and blessings. Some of us are more comfortable and familiar with particular states of mind. However, thought is meant to flow through them all, and using your mind effectively means finding the organic way your

There are two models of society—the dominator model involves the consciousness of ranking of some of humanity over the rest, symbolized by a blade and the power to take rather than give life as the ultimate power to establish and enforce domination. The second, when social relations are based on the consciousness of linking, is the partnership model, symbolized by a chalice, life generating and nurturing powers of the universe.

—Riane Eisler,
The Chalice and the Blade

brain sifts experience through the spiral of thinking. It also means becoming aware of the specific sequence your brain uses to trigger and access each state of consciousness. It is to that exploration we now turn.

Man seeks for himself, in whatever manner is suitable for him, a simplified and lucid image of the world, and so to overcome the world of experience by striving to replace it to some extent by this image.

—Albert Einstein

CHAPTER 3

THE NATURAL LANGUAGES OF YOUR MIND

Before working with architects, I had been intimately involved with psychiatrists and psychoanalytic schools as well as diplomats. Both are highly verbal and depend for their livelihood and their status on adeptness with spoken words. They can take words, and translate them into ideas and even emotions. One has to use words well if one wants to communicate with either group. Having become habituated to words after working with these two professions, my first contact with architects came as a shock. It was like working with an entirely new tribe about which I knew nothing. I learned that one had to reach this group through their eyes with pictures, not words.

—Edward Hall, *Beyond Culture*

This chapter is concerned with discovering which symbolic languages your mind uses to receive and organize information, balance inner and outer experience, and create new patterns from it.

People develop different sensory modalities either by temperament or training.... A.R. Luria discovered that the different centers of the brain are processing and contexting centers, not storage depots... They classify and context, pump information in and out but do not store it.... Karl Pribram of Stanford University was the first to build a theory of memory using the holographic model. He found it impossible to localize memory.... Visual and auditory imaging and memory have been extensively studied using a variety of techniques. However, other forms of memory have been neglected.

—Edward T. Hall, *Beyond Culture*

Have you ever wondered why some people are fascinated with lectures and concerts while others fall asleep in them? Or why, for some people, seeing is believing while for others, actions speak louder than words? Thirty years ago, working with children that had been labeled as disabled, I was very curious as to why some of them could learn to read if they walked around, but not if they sat still, and others had no trouble with spelling if they could sing the words they had to memorize instead of write them down. This wondering became a personal obsession that led me to realize that the distinct states of consciousness we employ in thinking were actually being **triggered** by the different symbolic languages the brain uses to process information—auditory (A), visual (V), kinesthetic (K).

When I began training in hypnotherapy, I had many opportunities to observe people as they changed from one level of thought to another—from fully alert consciousness, for instance, to daydreaming subconsciousness, to deeply entranced unconsciousness. I noticed that the language they used to describe what was going on in their minds, the images and symbols, frequently changed as their states of consciousness changed. It was like being in a house where the people spoke Italian in the living room, but as they moved through the hallway into the kitchen, they began to speak in Spanish, and by the time they got back into the bedroom everyone would *parler Français*. Each state of consciousness—beta, alpha, theta—seemed to use a different one of the three symbolic languages for processing information (auditory or visual or kinesthetic).

Before exploring this further, let's be explicit about what these different symbolic languages are. Thinking kinesthetically means functioning through hands, skin, and muscles. Experiences are collected in feelings, movements, actions, touch, texture, temperature, pressure, spatial awareness, sensitivity to energy, smell, and what I call "feelages"—internal images of movement and feeling. Creating kinesthetically involves using hands and bodies to sculpt, garden, dance, knit, carve, cook, mime, build, etc.

Thinking visually means functioning using your eyes and "insight" as the windows of your mind. Experience is processed through sight and visual images. When a mind is thinking this way, it's observing visual details, colors, visions, lines, maps, lists, views, perspectives, visualizations, drawings, the written word, diagrams, movies, charts, doodles, blueprints, television, photographs, wardrobes. Creating visually involves setting ideas to paper, canvas, or film.

Thinking auditorily means functioning using your ears and mouth as the telephone of your mind. Experience is processed through words and sounds. When a mind is thinking this way, it's listening to and participating in conversations, innuendos, tones of voice, jokes, jingles and sounds, music, meanings and messages, poems, stories, debates, speeches, orders, and orations, noise, radios and tape recorders, opera, lectures, and arguments. Creating auditorily involves expressing consciousness with sound and/or words.

Minds that don't change are like clams that don't open.
—Ursula LeGuin,
Dancing at the Edge of the World

Let's consider a thought to be like water. If you don't think about it very much, water is something you wash with or drink or use to brush your teeth. But if you consider it a little more deeply, you'll realize that water changes form constantly, evaporating into clouds, pouring on your umbrella, rushing down a mountainside into the stream that feeds the spring behind your house. It's still water, but it changes form.

In my experience, thought also changes form as it moves through the brain from one state of consciousness to another. Most of us who are familiar with computers understand that they use different kinds of language, such as FORTRAN, PASCAL, BASIC, etc., to process information. What makes the human mind so fascinating is that it uses three different perceptual "languages" to think. They seem to serve as a filing system for recording, sorting, creating, and retrieving thought, ideas, and experience.

As your mind moves a thought from conscious, to subconscious, to unconscious, *it changes the language or software it is using to think in each way.* You might, for example, hear some news on the radio and describe its meaning to yourself (consciously and auditorily); your mind then changes that explanation into a picture as it sorts the information to make it relevant to you (subconsciously and visually); and lastly, you space out for a moment or two as you lose track of the outside world, and remember a similar experience you had of what they were talking about on the broadcast (unconsciously and kinesthetically). If you stay in that state of mind, it may spin a web, connecting you to other feelings and actions, such as the first time you ever felt that way. None of these is actually "the thought." What is important is *how the thought is moving through your mind.*

What was most surprising to me when I first began to work with this information was that each symbolic language seems to trigger different states of consciousness in different people. Let's go into the office for an example. Jim is talking to his sales team about their plans for next year. Rose seems to be right with every word, poised on the edge of her chair, ready to ask and answer the next question. Bud, on the other hand, is drawing an intricate maze on the top yellow sheet of paper in his tablet, and Dave is motionless, staring out of the window, apparently not paying any attention at all. Jim may get very frustrated thinking that Dave is not paying attention or that what he is saying is boring. He doesn't realize that each of these people is in a different state of consciousness, digesting what he is saying differently, and that the way he is presenting information may be triggering those different ways of thinking.

Rose, listening so intently, is **consciously** taking the information in, "thinking" about the details that are being presented, asking the questions she needs in order to understand what is being said. Bud, with his doodling, is processing what he is hearing **subconsciously,** sorting through the information to figure out how it is relevant to him. Dave, staring out the window, is being triggered into theta consciousness by Jim's words. He may be thinking about last year's sales or wondering what they could do to sail through the competition. No one way of thinking is better than the other. No one member of the team is more attentive. Each of them is being influenced by Jim's verbal presentation into thinking about the information in different ways.

An understanding of how the two hemispheres process information is useful in considering approaches to teaching and learning, but in analyzing how individuals learn, relate, function and solve problems, identifying specific learning styles offers a more flexible approach.

—Linda V. Williams,
 *Teaching For the Two
 Sided Mind*

Symbolic Languages of Thinking

	KINESTHETIC	VISUAL	AUDITORY

Receive by: (input)	smelling
	tasting
	feeling
	sensing
	being touched
		watching TV,
		  movies
		reading
		viewing
		being shown
			listening to radio,
			  concerts
			attending lectures
			hearing
			being told

Imagery created: (internal process)	feelages
	sensations
	"inner dance" of
	  the mind
		insight
		visualizations,
		  visions
		"drive-in movies"
		  of the mind
			inner voice, self-
			  talk
			inner music
			"radio programs"
			  of the mind

Express by: (output)	handcrafting
	building
	driving
	gardening
	touching
	nursing
	"hands-on" healing
	clowning
	moving
	dancing
	participating in
	  sports
		writing
		editing
		drawing
		doodling
		designing
		painting
		creating graphics,
		  films,
		  lists,
		  charts,
		  diagrams
			speaking
			storytelling
			singing
			selling
			telling jokes
			discussing
			lecturing
			arguing
			philosophizing
			creating music

The Symbolic Languages of the Conscious Mind

You can begin to notice how your mind is triggered into different states of consciousness by exploring the ways you respond to simple things. If the above team members walk into another room of their office, for example, the first thing Rose is apt to be most attentive to is the conversation going on around her, since auditory stimulation is what triggers her conscious mind. Bud looks around to see what draws him visually since that is what triggers his beta consciousness, and Dave will probably be most attentive to what everyone is doing—since kinesthetic input triggers his conscious mind.

The symbolic language that triggers the conscious mode of thought is the one we find the most comfortable, and feel the most confident and competent using in expressing ourselves publicly. People think of it as "normal," as reality. It is both the one we need to use first so we can absorb information, and the symbology that makes us think we've fully remembered what we've learned. It is the "ON" switch for our brains, the nozzle for the hose that directs the stream of our attention. For each of us a particular language—visual, kinesthetic, auditory—sparks this state.

It's "normal" (or habitual) for me to paint a picture with the vocabulary of my *visual* conscious mind, for Andy, my husband, to communicate in feelings or action (*kinesthetic*), and for our friend Virginia to tell you in no uncertain terms exactly what she thinks are the underlying reasons for any given experience (*auditory*). If you met the three of us coming out of the same movie, you'd know all of the dialogue from Virginia, the action from Andy, and the visual descriptions from me.

I'd like to describe some other people to you and see if you recognize what their mind is doing to think in the organizing beta mode. Have you ever known anyone who could talk and talk and talk as if they could go on forever? They use language in very detailed ways. They may speak quickly. Their vocabulary may be very precise. Discussing something may seem very customary to them. The first thing they are attracted to walking in a room is the conversations that are going on. They know you care about them if you discuss things with them, particularly things that matter.

Different students remember and integrate information with different sensory modalities.

—Edward T. Hall,
Beyond Culture

Perhaps there's somebody else in your life who is a list maker, who loves crossword puzzles or doodling or using visual information to become very attentive—they're all eyes. How they dress, how they look to the rest of the world is very important to them. The first thing they do when they walk in a room is look around. They make direct and persistent eye contact. They can work at visually detailed tasks for a long time, and know you care about them if you show them or if they can see it in your face.

Have you ever known anyone who is very active? Physically it seems as if they can never sit still, they're always jiggling and wiggling, always doing something, playing with something in their hands. Their whole orientation to life is hands on. In fact, they cannot "think" coherently unless they are in movement, action, or experiencing tactile stimulation. They feel their way through the world. When they enter a room where a party is being held, they'll probably feel where the energy is most comfortable for them. They organize their life in piles. The way they do things is very systematic. The way they feel things can be very systematic. They like things concrete, and being of use in the world is what's important to them. They know you care about them by how you touch them and do things with them.

Hopefully, you may have also recognized yourself in one of those three different ways of thinking consciously. Most likely, you recognized other people in your life as well. But let's begin with noticing you. Which of those ways of concentrating seems most familiar to you, most real, most natural?

One way to think of this mode is as the high threshold of concentration. A threshold used to be the place in a doorway where the wheat was laid. When a wind came along, it would blow away the chaff and retain the grain. Thus, if someone has a high threshold, the winds of distraction have a hard time disturbing them. Can you be engaged in a conversation for a very long time, and even if you are interrupted, go right back to what you were talking about? If you are what a friend of mine calls "word smart," we can say that you have a high auditory threshold.

On the other hand, if you are "body smart," and have a high

> Ah, if you could dance all that you've just said, then I'd understand.
>
> —Nikos Kazantakis,
> *Zorba the Greek*

kinesthetic threshold, you can do a task logically, concentrating on it for long periods of time. Even if you have to leave it, you can come right back to the place you stopped. If your conscious mind is triggered kinesthetically, touch would not distract you. In fact, it would seem quite casual.

Perhaps you have a high visual threshold, you're "visually smart," and you can make lists forever, organizing yourself precisely this way. You can sit at your desk writing or drawing or reading and nothing can disturb you. Possibly, you can read and watch TV at the same time. If you are momentarily distracted from a visual task, you can go right back to concentrating on it.

Spend the afternoon.
You can't take it with you.

—Annie Dillard

Practice: Getting to the Point

Time to get wet again. Even if you think you are sure which symbolic language triggers your conscious mind, this practice will give you the opportunity to swim in it. I invite you to use the same curiosity you usually reserve for strangers or a first date:

- Begin by noticing what you are most aware of in the present moment for several minutes. You might want to say it out loud or tape record where your attention leads you. Keep it simple—just the information that your senses give you, e.g., "I'm looking at the fuchsia wallpaper," rather than "I see the wallpaper and I wonder what store it was purchased in, and whether it's vinyl or grasscloth. It reminds me of the wall paper my Aunt Sylvia had when I was little…"

- Now, a question to think about. Please write or tape record your response. "How do you know when someone loves you?"

- Notice the sensory quality of your description, e.g., "I know because of the way someone **talks** to me, the **tone of voice** she uses, his or her engagement when we **discuss** ideas."

- Which symbolic language do you feel the most confident in using?

Was one very difficult to access or not available to you?

Kindred Clubs

No one wants to be pigeonholed, and no one wants to be thought of as being just like anyone else. Yet there is frequently a delightful sense of coming home, and of being profoundly understood when people in our workshops cluster together with others whose conscious minds are triggered by the same symbolic language. It's much like being in an orchestra with similar instruments tuning up. In order for you to have a bit of that experience, I've woven together some excerpts of actual comments from "kinclubs" of the three different conscious perceptual persuasions. So that you can enter the experience, pretend you have no idea what triggers your mind into organizing information. Imagine you are visiting each group, eavesdropping, observing, getting a feel for which one might be kin to your mind.

Please remember that within each group there is tremendous variation, because your mind is a unique instrument. There may be some things you recognize and others that you don't.

Selfishness is not living as one wishes to live; it is asking others to live as one wishes to live.

—Ruth Rendell

Does This Sound True?

Those whose conscious minds are auditorily attuned establish verbal rapport very quickly. There is almost no silence between words. They seem to get friendly by joking around, saying things they call "just kidding." They are often sarcastic, but don't seem to take offense at someone else's words. There is a lot of discussion of reasons and meanings, understandings, and personal philosophies.

"I can talk **to** anybody about anything. I talk to people in elevators, on street corners, wherever. But looking at them means I have to take them in somehow. That's more intimate, and I have a harder time finding words. Touching I save for special situations.

"So does this mean my brain works like Robin Williams'? I always secretly thought I was Robin Williams' long lost sister, stolen at birth by a Lithuanian white slave trader who...."

"And by the way, you forgot to ask me how I know if someone loves me. I can tell from their conversation; from their level of attention as we talk; if they call me up to talk things over, like ideas or opinions; if they really listen and enjoy my jokes, stories, and poems; and of course if they stay up late into the night with me, discussing something I'm excited about, then ZONGO! I know."

We meet ourselves time and again in a thousand disguises on the path of life.
—Carl Jung

"I get very upset if I don't remember someone's name. I also hate to hear criticism, but I can talk so much no one else gets a chance to get a word in edgewise. When I meet someone, I'm most aware of what they are saying, and I think over quite carefully how I will present myself in words. Music relaxes me, and I love talk shows on the radio. I've often fantasized about starting one."

"People used to say I was vaccinated with a phonograph needle. I like to be boss and give orders, I really do. I talked to this woman who was a judge and I just talked at her until I got my way. Once I start I don't stop. I'd probably be a good auctioneer."

"Do you like to argue? I like to debate, not fight exactly, but philosophically discuss things. I can talk on for days about what something means. That's the only way to resolve differences... communication is everything. I hate it when someone gives me the silent treatment—I go up the wall. I like to process things. As soon as I walk out of a movie, I need to talk about it."

Does This Feel Comfortable?

Those who are body smart usually stand and rock, or sit close to each other and jiggle. In a New York workshop, after ten minutes, these folks had taken off their shoes and were rubbing each others' feet as they spoke. They dress for comfort. Often they have what is called a "flat affect"— their faces don't show very much of what is really going on for them; it is their bodies that communicate their mental energy.

"I'm feeling the floor under my ankles and a place where my shoulder is tense. I'm smelling something being cooked in the kitchen and feeling the breeze on my face. I'm aware of how people are moving in the room, and I feel myself rocking back and forth, feel my voice vibrating in my throat.

"I'd be much more comfortable doing things with you all, walking, making things, or maybe, if I knew you, sitting next to you silently and touching you. And oh yes, I know someone cares about me because I can feel it. Especially if they touch me or do something with me. It's just a sense I have. The energy gets charged, sometimes electric, and I get goose bumps and tingles."

"Let's not sit down, please. I've been going stir crazy sitting in this room for the last half hour. What I'm mostly noticing is the energy in the room. I find it much more interesting than anything else. I often get distracted by it, as a matter of fact, if I'm supposed to be sitting still paying attention to words."

"I always want to touch people when I talk to them. I want to reach out, it comes naturally to me, and it gets me in trouble all the time, because people always misinterpret why I'm touching them. It's very painful to me, because it's the most comfortable way for me to communicate, and if someone freaks out, I figure I did something wrong."

See Anyone Who Resembles You?

Those whose beta consciousness is triggered by visual input seem to leave enough space between themselves so they can see one another while they talk. Movements are minimal, except for heads and hands. When one person is talking, all the heads turn in that direction. There is persistent eye contact, and facial expressions are very explicit. These people often are very carefully dressed and color–coordinated. Many of them take notes or doodle.

"I'm aware of seeing the tree outside the window; I'm noticing the people inside the room getting comfortable by moving around; I'm

Turn up the lights. I don't
want to go home in
the dark.
—O. Henry, last words

looking at my hands now… I'm noticing the colors of the clothes that people are wearing. I'm seeing little details like the buttons on his shirt and the barrettes in her hair. I'm noticing the pattern on the rug, the blue and red, seeing the sunlight and shadows on the wall.

"I know someone loves me immediately by their facial expression. I can read faces like I read books or photographs. And I know if they show me, with notes and letters, or presents. Of course I also know I'm cared about if I'm noticed wearing a new sweater, for example. If someone wants to see the photographs I take or something I've written, I really feel loved."

"One of the things that's always been important to me is eye contact. If people don't look at me when I'm talking to them, I feel erased, as if they don't like me. I make eye contact in every situation first thing. If someone is evading my eyes, I feel as if that person doesn't want to know me. Color is everything to me, and I read the world. Cereal boxes, chewing gum wrappers, faces, graffiti; my eyes never seem to rest. It's as if they're my windows to the world."

"I'm very concerned about the way I look—appearances seem to be everything. I just assume it's the first thing on everyone's mind. I need people to show me they love me: give me something I can see, send me written words, cards, flowers. Seeing is believing. How I'm seen obsesses me sometimes. How my car looks, my wife, my body, even my dog!"

"The written word is very important to me. It's so much easier for me to learn when there's something for me to look at. If I can't see, I can't hear."

"People say they can always tell what's going on for me just by taking one look at me. I guess that's true, I wear my heart on my face."

Practice for Expanding Your Learnings

- *Pick a word, an interesting one such as "passion," and ask as many people as you'd like to describe it to you. Note their perceptual differences.*

Choosing Your Path

Recently, as awareness has begun to grow that we have different "styles" of learning, I've been hearing some people say, "Oh, that's because I'm a visual person." Or, "I have to talk a lot because I'm an auditory learner." This is as inaccurate as someone saying, "I'm a left-brained person." Or as incomplete as it would be to identify a Stradivarius by saying "It's a stringed instrument." That doesn't help you know whether you should use a bow or strum the instrument to play it. To call yourself a visual learner only describes what triggers your mind into the most focused state, what brings you into beta consciousness so you can concentrate in that one way. Each thinking instrument receives and uses visual, auditory, and kinesthetic information, but for thinking in a different mode and in different sequences.

In learning how you learn, the next logical step would be to uncover the symbolic language used by your subconscious mind. But thousands of people have taught me that understanding how we learn does not always follow the steps that the conscious mind deems logical. Because it is so sensitive, many people find that they are more aware of how their unconscious mind is triggered than their subconscious mind. I have decided therefore to include it next, "out of order." If this is difficult for you, please feel free to jump ahead to the next section and then back to here. There are also some who, once they can identify the trigger to their conscious mind, want immediately to jump to uncovering their pattern. If this is true for you, by all means, follow your own inclination and go directly to the next chapter, returning to this section when you are ready.

> We shall not cease from exploration and the end of all our exploring will be to arrive where we started and know the place for the first time.
>
> —T.S. Eliot

The Symbolic Language of the Unconscious Mind

Moving to the outermost part of the spiral where your mind is triggered into producing more theta waves, we come to your unconscious mind. (Actually, to be precise, the outermost ring of the spiral should be reserved for where your mind produces the most delta waves, but that area of the unconscious mind is where sleep occurs, and thus, not in the realm of this book.)

There is nothing wrong with you. Anyone who says something is wrong is wrong.

—Rennais Jeanne Hill

Because the theta state is so receptive, it is the one with which your mind receives the world most deeply, yet you have the least awareness of these images (which may be visual, auditory, or kinesthetic). They are the most dim, the farthest away, the hardest to hear. They are also the most childlike and unusual.

That's because it takes longer for material to come into your present awareness when it originates in this region of your mind. I'm thinking of a large bear who has been hibernating, and lumbers from the deepest part of the cave blinking, scratching, and growling to the opening and the light. The unconscious mind is where there is the lowest threshold of concentration—meaning literally where the most wind can blow through. Thus, here we are both the most open and the most distractible.

The unconscious mind has a major input function: to connect one thing with another, and a major output function: to generate and express the distilled experiences of your life in new patterns. When an event is taken in deeply in the symbolic language of your unconscious mind—the sight of a homeless person in the streets, the sound of an animal howling in fear, the feeling of a woman in pain confined to a hospital bed—you connect to it as if it is happening to you. You go through your own life to find a similar experience. If you take that connection as inspiration, the energy will weave or dance or carve or sing or write itself outward into the world. (You may not have any awareness of inspiration in the symbolic language of your unconscious mind, particularly if you spend most of your time with a very active attention. By the time you "get" it, it has been translated into alpha or beta symbology.)

Have you ever known anyone who is "eye shy," who seems to

have great difficulty maintaining direct eye contact for any length of time? Those whose unconscious minds think visually may be highly affected by movies or other visual input, since they become what they see. They may ignore visual details, for what matters to them is the "larger picture," seeing the whole of something. They might describe this way of thinking as disappearing into what they see, the colors bleeding together as if seen through a rain-splattered window.

Visually sensitive minds tend to dislike detailed written instructions, and long written reports. Because the threshold is low here, a pile of papers to be read or written may be overwhelming. When these people do write something, it usually has great meaning to them.

Perhaps you can think of someone whose unconscious mind has a low auditory threshold. He or she probably gets easily overloaded with too many words. Names, acronyms, and verbal content may be forgotten, but a tone of voice will be remembered for years. Usually people whose minds are auditorily sensitive can be easily distracted by being spoken to, or by people filling in words for their unfinished sentences.

Silence is the greatest gift to them, because the most generative aspect of their minds is continually assaulted with words from the outside. They may not speak easily or quickly, or they may speak quite rapidly, their words seeming to pinwheel, making apparently unrelated connections. When their words or music do emerge from a comfortable silence, they can hold great wisdom and have a profound effect on listeners. In addition, they have the capacity to hear melody and harmonies at the same time, as well as to listen to the whole of a conversation.

Is there someone you know with a low kinesthetic threshold? They will be easily distracted by touch and a lot of movement around them. People whose unconscious minds think kinesthetically may "space out" and be very cautious about being touched or being taught how to do physical things. They may also sabotage (unconsciously of course) any attempt to compete physically by being injured or accident prone. Kinesthetically sensitive minds feel things very deeply, but take a long time to know what they are

The Blues is the truth. You'd better believe that what they're telling you is the truth.

—Buddy Guy

actually feeling. It may seem as if they can sit still forever, inactive, even forgetting they are in a body.

People whose minds process information this way may get lost in movement, because they start doing one thing and then naturally begin to get "creative" and do it another way and then another in no apparent logical order. An unconscious mind that is triggered by kinesthetic input feels the whole of something, and is not casual about touch since it will remember that touch for a long time.

Kindred Clubs

What follows are excerpts of actual comments from theta mode "kin-clubs" of the three perceptual persuasions. You may recognize characteristics that will help you identify your own.

Auditorily Sensitive

The most outstanding thing about people whose unconscious minds are triggered like this is that they seem to ask each other continual questions that often are never answered. They frequently display discomfort at having the rest of us listen to them.

"I hate it when other people ask me yes/no questions. I always feel as if I'm on the spot and the words just don't come. Whatever I say hardly touches what I'm feeling. I can hear myself answer in 50 different ways before the words leave my lips. Then I'm never satisfied with what I finally do say. Did you ever go through that?"

"I get trapped by the voices in my head. Maybe they're trying to block out everyone else. I'm learning here that when someone puts me down with words, those words remain in my mind for a long time."

"I get addicted to very dogmatic, articulate speakers. I was in a group with this leader who was verbally very powerful. I had to call her on the telephone three times a day, and listen to her while sitting still in

Current research seems to be indicating that each cell can also carry memory and think.

—Ernest Rossi & David B. Cheek, *Mind Body Therapy*

meetings. Her voice became like a drug and I was like a junkie. Her words kept coming out of my mouth instead of my own. This went on for two years! From what I now know, that's pretty common. We get hooked easily to powerful speakers who say things in a linear way that our brains can't. They have such organized explanations for things, don't they?"

Visually Sensitive

The distinguishing characteristic among people whose unconscious minds are visually triggered is that they don't like to look at other people for very long.

"Eye contact is torture for me. When I look down or away, which is what I need to do to be present and feel myself, people act as if I'm a four year old or tell me I'm shifty. If I make steady eye contact I go blank and limp or stone-eyed. The looks on other people's faces tell me so much. But I have to be careful reading people, because often I slip into my own movies and lose the person I'm with all together."

"I love the descriptive scenes in novels, when they write so I can see the whole environment, but the dialogue bores me. I tend to be a very slow reader, or else skim over the surface, getting an overview of the whole book. It's also important how a particular word looks— that's how I spell, by the shape of the word."

"I used to hate it when teachers wrote all over my spelling tests. It looked like the paper was bleeding. And why did they have to put on those dumb faces and how many wrong I got in big letters? Even in college, when they wrote comments on the paper it was like they were writing on my flesh. My writing, being seen in general, feels like being naked, and being naked can be agonizing or exquisite, depending."

"I hate those guided visualizations, where I have to close my eyes. First of all, I get real frustrated because I see so many possibilities.

If you want to write the truth, you must write about yourself. I am the only real truth I know.

—Jean Rhys

They say, 'See a castle and a road' and I see variations of every kind of castle that's ever been built. By that time, they're off onto something else. I hate having visions imposed on me. It has to come from inside me. I hated that book where it told you what colors to wear for the same reasons. The visual images in my mind go very fast in a blur or I can't see them at all unless I slow down. Then they become very real, as if I'm in them."

Kinesthetically Sensitive

The distinguishing characteristic among these people is the space they place between each other and the absence of any movement. When they talk about their bodies or feelings, they often giggle nervously or lower their voices and lean in.

"I hate to learn physical things like ballroom dancing or sports in a structured manner. I always get bored, or mess up and do it my own way. I took a lot of dance classes so I could learn to move like everyone else, but there was always something in me that resented being told how I was supposed to do it. They would skip and hop to the right and I'd find myself going to the left. I felt erased if I moved just like everyone else."

"I had a love/hate thing with competitive sports. My dad wanted me to play football. I had to go very numb to make my dad proud. I got very disciplined. It was ego gratifying to have the cheerleaders shout for me, but I had to put myself through a lot. I'm sweating as I talk about it. Two years ago I went to Alaska and got frostbitten all over, but I didn't even know it. Endure, overcome. I feel very sad now thinking about all of that enduring I did."

"I'm not in my body too much. When I was a kid and got beat up by my parents, I'd just leave my body and watch the whole thing from inside of the wall. That way the deepest part of me never got beat up. The trouble is, I not only distanced myself from the pain, I also distanced myself from myself. It's still hard to crawl back into my body. Other people keep saying 'I feel tingly.' Well, I don't feel

—but it is always living, moving, and your mind is like that. It is In the flowing river there are so many things—fishes, leaves, dead animals everlastingly restless, flitting from one thing to another like a butterfly—just watch your mind. It is great fun. If you try it as fun as an amusing thing, you will find that the mind begins to settle down without any effort on your part to control it.

—J. Krishnamurti,
Think On These Things

all of those things in my body. I keep waiting. 'When is the tingle gonna start? Was that it? Nah, just my imagination.'"

"Getting sick was the only way I could get receptive to my own body sensations. That also forced me to get creative and begin to draw so I'd have something to do, some way to communicate with what I was feeling. My body talks to me, but I've only recently learned that it has certain ways it says no, with pain and tension, and other ways it says yes, with pleasure and easing. Checking in with my body takes so long. My visual and verbal ideas move so much faster."

> A poem...begins as a lump in the throat, a sense of wrong, a homesickness, a lovesickness.... It finds the thought and the thought finds the words.
>
> —Robert Frost

Messages from Your Unconscious Mind: The Doodle Bug

Most of us have been educated to think of ourselves as "uncreative" and fail to notice the humming, doodling, and gesturing that may, in fact, be hidden analogies for creative ways of thinking about the same old thing.

Carlos sat in every session of the Vermont training group creating intricate doodles. He was a wonderful athlete, coach, and science teacher, but he insisted that he was neither intuitive nor creative. His major issue in life was that he had difficulty remembering certain things, such as appointments. He procrastinated with all of his paperwork for school. He and his wife frequently fought over his "just disappearing," not showing up where and when he said he would. She called it "sneaking off."

His conscious mind, which he depended on quite heavily, was triggered by kinesthetic symbology. His unconscious mind, which he largely discounted, was visually sensitive. When I asked about his doodles, he dismissed them as an outlet for his energy when he got bored listening to lectures. I questioned him about what we had been discussing in session that morning. He shrugged, his facial muscles flattening, and said he had no idea.

"Carlos, do me a favor, even though it may seem odd to you. Trace back over the doodle you were doing this morning, and notice what comes into your mind."

He got one of those this-woman-must-be-crazy looks, and

mumbled, "I don't get what this has to do with anything." But he did begin to retrace through the ornate and primal doodle.

After two minutes, in a dream-like voice, he said, "Well, you talked about hypnosis, but... oh yeah, then Alan said that trance and meditation are not really the same, because..."

He reported **everything** that had been said, in this casually dazed way, for ten full minutes before I stopped him. He was more surprised than I was.

I suggested that his doodling was communication from his intuition, bringing experience to him in the visual language of his unconscious mind. He shook his head in disbelief, and turned the page, beginning to retrace the doodle he had "mindlessly" done. "I just cannot... believe... this. It **is** working. I am remembering what you said."

He looked at me with the innocent wonder of a six year old. "All of these years I have been throwing out my doodles, throwing out my intuition! Why didn't anyone tell me? Do you know how much I have suffered in school trying to remember?"

I did know.

• • •

You too are getting continual messages from your unconscious mind. Perhaps, while thinking about a fight you had with someone at the office, you find yourself "spacing out," remembering the feeling of a roller coaster ride you took when you were seven, and how you couldn't get off even when you wanted to. Are you willing to consider that in the tomb of your mind is a message that you are relating to this person as though you were trapped in a roller coaster?

Does a song just "pop" into your mind as you are pacing in your kitchen? Does your hand keep making a fist while you are trying to decide how much more you should give to an abusing friend? It may be irrelevant, but then again, it may be your unconscious mind offering you a seed, a possibility, another way.

One of the most significant and important aspects of understanding how your mind processes information comes with the realization that the state of consciousness that is most difficult to access,

My life in writing, or my life as a writer, comes to me as two parts, like two rivers that blend. One part is easy to tell: the times, the events, the places, the people. The other part is mysterious; it is my thoughts, the flow of my inner life, the reveries and impulses that never get known—perhaps even to me.

—William Stafford,
You Must Revise Your Life

your unconscious mind, is the source of your personal creativity and generativity. What you may experience as the most "private" state of mind, the most frustrating, the least "brilliant" and competitive is, in fact, the storehouse for all you have ever experienced. It is the generating station for your wisdom and guidance, and the ultimate navigator of your life's path.

I have worked with thousands of people who have reclaimed their right to express and explore their imagination as a process for healing their lives and making sense of what could not be rationally understood. They make their living working as teachers, scientists, carpenters. They make their lives by finding truth in their music, their stories, the crafts of their hands.

> The fabled musk deer searches the world over for the source of the scent which comes from itself.
>
> —Ramakrishna

Practice:
A Creative Approach to Problem Solving

- *Bring a problem you are having to mind and describe it in your habitual way.*

- *Using your non-dominant hand, draw a line that depicts what the problem is like, doodle its shape, even color it if you choose.*

- *Shift to the kinesthetic mode and let your hand describe the problem in the way it moves.*

- *Vocalize it in humming, making sounds so that the energy in your voice rather than the language describes the problem.*

- *With all of this in mind, make up a story that begins, "Once upon a time…" Change the context so that it's "Once upon a time a gnarly elm tree was struck by lightning … ," rather than, "Once upon a time a woman had a terrible day…"*

What your unconscious mind has just given you is a map of a new way to approach the problem, not a solution. At first you may not understand it, but then how does one understand a map? Just notice the effect the story has on you in the next few days.

The Symbolic Language of Your Subconscious Mind

I never used to spend much time teaching about the subconscious mind. If the truth be known, I didn't find it very interesting. Nothing much seemed to happen there. I was concerned with intense action, or complete relaxation. My head was in the clouds, full of visions, my feet were deeply rooted by the feeling of gravity in the ground, and what was in between seemed basically irrelevant. The fact that I spent so much time with words, the triggering language of my subconscious mind in my day-to-day life, was very confusing to me.

Someone in a Boston supervision group challenged me about this: "Why don't we ever have kinclubs to explore alpha consciousness? We've done beta and theta, and overall patterns, but you always leave the subconscious mind out. How come?"

I blushed in embarrassment and recognition of the truth, and then agreed to have alpha kinclubs. I expected it would be the most boring of all our sessions. I was wrong—grossly, outrageously wrong! At the end of the day, one of the participants shouted, "Dawna, our whole lives revolve around these in-between minds. They're the middle third!"

She was right. Alpha is the bridging place between the inner and outer worlds. When our brains are producing more alpha waves, we are capable of splitting our attention to maintain an internal and external focus simultaneously. For example, in this moment, I'm hearing Barbra Streisand sing "Where Is It Written?" on the stereo downstairs. At the same time, a steady voice inside the left side of my skull is dictating the words I am typing. Both of these awarenesses coexist quite comfortably.

I cannot, however, see the little black letters bounce across the screen and simultaneously see an image inside my mind. Nor can I walk quickly around the room while feeling deep sensations in my body. It is only in my auditory channel that input from the inner world and the outer world can be processed together.

You might take a moment right now to find which symbolic language you can pay attention to internally and externally at the same

The corpus callosum function is to provide communication between the two hemispheres and allow transmission of memory and learning.

—Roger Sperry, CIT, psychobiologist, quoted in *Drawing on the Right Side of the Brain*

time, naturally and easily.

People whose sorting mode uses the kinesthetic channel might need to move, act, use their hands, or connect with their feelings in order to get unstuck in puzzling situations. Fear leaves them paralyzed, and they frequently experience worry as a churning sensation in their bodies. Other people often describe themselves as being a sports car at a stop light with the engine revving high, because they always seem to have a pent-up energy right beneath the surface. This sometimes produces what one person called "the syndrome of the emotional athlete," a very apt phrase because athletics and movement can help people whose minds operate in this way to balance and direct all the intense energy they are aware of.

The highest human capacity is the capacity for metaphor.

—Aristotle

People whose subconscious mode uses the visual channel might use writing, drawing, or photography to clarify things when they are confused. Their lives may revolve around being seen or seeing (such as working on a computer, in a ledger book, on a stage), showing, and demonstrating. They tend to experience fear as being blank or having a blind spot, and worry as quickly flashing images. They can see visual images with their eyes open and usually in three dimensions, and discuss them quite easily. This is not the case for their feelings, however. It may be much easier for them to write about their feelings (or draw them) than discuss them directly.

For those whose alpha thinking is triggered by the auditory channel, talking to other people helps eliminate confusion. Their words are not necessarily detailed, though, and tend to involve narrating stories about their experience or using metaphors to describe inner feelings or visions. Their words often carry a lot of vocal energy and variation, which makes them naturally powerful teachers, no matter what their vocation. They often learn as they teach. Fear leaves them speechless, and worry is experienced by them as an incessant inner dialogue.

They frequently find themselves in dialogue between people, translating what one is saying to another, using words to bridge the gaps.

The Middle Third Kinclubs

In these kinclubs, people neither slipped into an immediate rapport as they did in the gatherings of the conscious mind, nor entered into a sacred kind of union as they did in those of the unconscious mind. It was as if they were at the same station waiting for different trains. What was most interesting was how people seemed to use that "alpha language" to facilitate their thinking.

Visually Centered

"I seem to be able to see the whole of something as well as the details. I never noticed that before, but it's true. I do have problems talking about my feelings—what I experience in my body—unless I spend some time writing about them first. It helps condense everything down."

"I can see images with my eyes open or closed. If I'm having a hard time, I may actually be in a very dramatic movie in my head without even knowing it. Sometimes, when I'm really furious or confused, the only thing that helps is to walk around and notice the visual details of the world. That brings me into the present and calms me down."

"Strange. I don't seem to feel a whole lot. But if I see someone else feeling something, then I'm into it with them. I also seem to have to do whatever I see. Having a blank wall in front of me helps me to concentrate."

"I see both sides of every issue—sometimes simultaneously! Looking at things in nature helps me balance in a certain way. Reading also takes me far away, which is why I love it so. When I'm in bed with my husband and I look at him, I only can find him, but if I look out through our skylight at the stars, I'm found again."

"If I make a picture in my mind of some pleasant place in my mind, my whole body relaxes and I'm there for a moment. This works

Perhaps [we] would do well to lose the plan, throw away the map, get off the motorcycle, put on a very strange-looking hat, bark sharply three times, and trot off looking thin, yellow, and dingy across the desert and up into the digger pines.... We're in a rational dilemma, an either/or situation as perceived by the binary computer mentality, and neither the either nor the or is a place where people can live.... I am offered the Grand Inquisitor's choice. Will you choose freedom without happiness, or happiness without freedom? The only answer one can make, I think, is: No.

—Ursula K. LeGuin, *Dancing at the Edge of the World*

really well in the dentist's chair. I also use a similar technique when I have to speak to a group of people. I just picture each one as a child, superimposed over their adult face, and the words flow out much more easily."

Kinesthetically Centered

"I'm always doing things. I like to stay in action. At first I thought this meant that my conscious mind was triggered by kinesthetic, but I think I am so active to keep sane and to help me sort out all I am thinking about. My mind runs away with me and movement actually relaxes me instead of waking me up the way it does those guys who are consciously kinesthetic. If I don't run or bike every day, I start to be a nervous wreck."

"Yeah, I work out before I sleep! I'm a business man with the feelings of a ballet dancer! They almost have a life of their own. If I stay very active, and go very fast, I don't feel them. Consequently, I almost never go slow."

"If I lose awareness of what I'm feeling, and stop dancing, which is my workout, I either get sick or injure myself in some way. My body is my barometer. If I'm feeling everyone else's feelings, I get sick. It's as if my body is trying to pull my mind back home. I love helping others talk about what they're feeling. My whole life revolves around that."

Auditorily Centered

"To become aware of what's really going on inside of me, I need to talk to someone about it. How I talk to myself in my mind makes all the difference in my entire mental state. I didn't trust my internal voice for a long time. It just kept going back and forth, back and forth. I couldn't tell if what I was hearing inside was my voice or something I'd heard from someone else in the past."

"I hate saying the same thing over and over, but sometimes I find

Crusaders for virtue are an awkward embarrassment to any society; they force us to make choices: either side with them, which is difficult and dangerous, or condemn them, which leads to self betrayal.

—Edward Abbey

myself doing just that because I realize I'm trying to sort things out or convince someone else—or myself. I also tell a lot of stories. My brain just spits them out naturally. People laugh at my metaphors, but I can't talk without them."

"I improvise when I talk to groups. If I memorize what I'm going to say, I sound like a zombie. My voice carries what I'm feeling. As soon as someone else talks, I know a lot about him or her in some kind of intuitive way I can't describe. It makes me crazy."

"If I've been around people with an accent for a while, I start talking just like them. Maybe that's why I write great dialogues. But when I want to write with my own voice, I need total or almost complete silence. I'm also afraid my words will hurt someone else. That's probably why I don't say things too definitively or in a straightforward fashion."

Chart of Triggers to States of Consciousness

Now is the time to say that charts help some people learn; but they just confuse others, because they see themselves in everything they read. If they confuse you, that may indicate that your subconscious mind is being triggered. Or maybe you only like charts that have very few words in them, preferring visual symbols. This may indicate that your unconscious mind is triggered by visual input. If you love the charts that follow, if they clarify everything for you, then perhaps like mine, your conscious mind is triggered by visual input.

Triggers to States of Consciousness

If Kinesthetic Activity Triggers:	If Auditory Activity Triggers:	If Visual Activity Triggers:
CONSCIOUS MIND • learns most easily by doing • immediate access of physical sensations • does things logically • movement is strong, direct • jiggles, constantly in motion • touch energizes, brings alert • touch is casual, natural • organizes in piles	**CONSCIOUS MIND** • learns most easily by discussing • immediate access of names, what was said • says things logically, no hesitation • describes abstract ideas with complex language • constant and intense talking • speaking energizes, brings alert • verbal contact is casual, natural • organizes by talking about what needs to be done	**CONSCIOUS MIND** • learns most easily by reading, watching • immediate access of the way things look • writes things logically • shows and illustrates ideas • constant and intense eye contact • writing energizes, brings alert • eye contact is casual, natural • organizes in lists
SUBCONSCIOUS MIND • movement helps to sort thoughts • feels pent-up energy frequently • feelings right beneath the surface • often pulled in two directions • hand gestures accompany words • feels what they see or hear • touch/movement is bridge between inner and outer worlds	**SUBCONSCIOUS MIND** • talking helps to sort thoughts • hears both sides of a story • metaphors right beneath the surface • can hear inner voice while listening to words on the outside • may hesitate slightly to find words • can hear the whole and details in a conversation • words are the bridge between inner and outer worlds	**SUBCONSCIOUS MIND** • writing/drawing helps to sort thoughts • sees things from two directions • visions right beneath the surface • can see visions with eyes open or closed • has to look to side to find words • can see whole and details • vision is bridge between inner and outer worlds
UNCONSCIOUS MIND • feels the whole of something • doesn't like to do things in the same way repeatedly • needs verbal or visual instructions to learn to do new things • needs to close eyes to access body sensations • feelings can be overwhelming • very sensitive and shy to touch • touch entrances • movement generates ideas • does things non-linearly, creatively	**UNCONSCIOUS MIND** • hears the whole of something • doesn't like to speak in detailed way to groups of people • may forget names, initials, words may take a long time to access • hates to have words filled in by others • words may be overwhelming • can hear harmonies internally • sensitive to tone of voice • auditory input entrances • sounds generate ideas • hears things creatively	**UNCONSCIOUS MIND** • sees the whole of something • doesn't like to write detailed things in the same way repeatedly • shy and sensitive to prolonged eye contact • visual stimulation can be overwhelming • visual input entrances • visions generate ideas • sees things creatively

Practice: Noticing How Life Affects You

- *Let's explore the natural choreography of your different states of consciousness from the inside out. We're not searching for your pattern, just notice whatever you can about what helps you refine, define and organize your thinking, sort out possibilities, and generate images. To discover what triggers different states of consciousness for you, begin by noticing connections. For instance, if you amble on a walk to no place in particular, or give yourself a foot rub, how is your mind affected? Does it expand or contract? How does kinesthetic input affect your state of consciousness?*

- *Now, I'd like to invite you to play some unfamiliar music—whatever you'd consider your favorite type, but new to you. Notice how listening affects your state of mind. What happens when you listen to the radio or to a lecture? How does this auditory input affect you?*

- *Lastly, visual input. When you read, or watch a movie, or wander around in a museum or a store where you aren't looking for anything in particular—just glancing around—what happens to the circumference of your mind? Does it expand or contract?*

- *When you review your responses to the above practice, notice how different input affected your consciousness: Which seemed to space you out the most, spread your mind wide as water, bring you deep inside, connect you to memories or metaphors?*

- *Which brought you the most alert, closest to your conscious mind, to a crisp awareness of the present outer reality?*

- *Which brought you to the "middle third," between internal and external awareness, balancing in both places?*

Typically, people float back and forth in these currents of thought without noticing where they are or what perceptual language is triggering their brain into a particular state of mind. If this practice has not left you certain about how your mind is processing information, just continue to notice yourself with curiosity and compassion. The chapters that follow will assist you in determining how to weave this

Tell me what you pay attention to and I will tell you who you are.

—Jose Ortega y Gasset

all together into your personal thinking pattern. Remember, it's all just practice!

CHAPTER 4

THE TRUE NATURE OF OUR DIFFERENCES

We are all so different largely because we all have different combinations of intelligences. If we recognize this, I think we will have at least a better chance of dealing appropriately with the many problems that we face in the world.

—Howard Gardner

This chapter presents you with an overview of the global skill this book is all about—discovering the personal thinking pattern your mind uses to access your natural intelligence. It offers several ways of finding out what that pattern is, what the value is of knowing it, and how to distinguish your thinking pattern from your personality.

Every person who has spent any time with children, or as a child, knows about individual differences. If you listen to parents in a park or teachers in a faculty lounge, it's not uncommon to hear comparisons such as "Sally is a climber, but Justin can be content to sit and watch the world go by." You hear them talking about the traits that make them endearing and those that drive them crazy—how Ted can't ever seem to sit still, how Rosita is always asking "Why," how Katie is so neat and tidy, how Reggie is the quiet one in the family, or how Lana has always been good with her hands. These simple, everyday things that make each child stand out are the kinds of characteristics that on a more sophisticated level will help you discover your own and others' thinking patterns.

Finding your pattern is not as complicated as it sounds. Consider yourself a detective, gathering many clues, digging deep into what you already know about yourself, and becoming aware of behaviors or traits you might have taken for granted. Consider this a fascinating adventure, one that will leave you saying, "Oh, so *that's* why!" As we have been discovering in the last chapter, each of the three consciousness levels is most sensitive to just one symbolic language. Consequently, there are six possible sequences your brain can use to process information: three possibilities for your conscious mind, or three different high thresholds as we just experienced. That leaves two for your subconscious mind. And that leaves one for your unconscious mind. So there are six different possibilities:

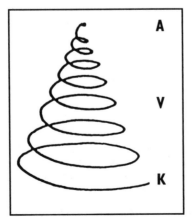

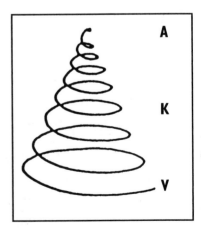

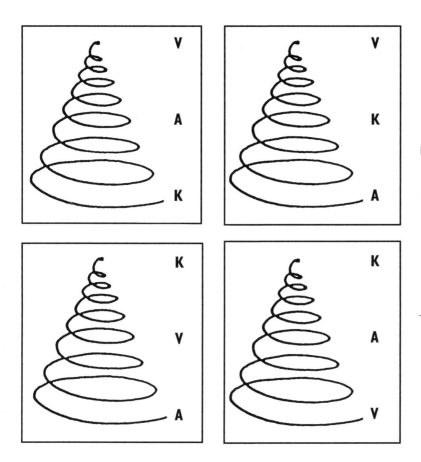

When we learn something, cells in many parts of the brain learn a new rhythm of firing corresponding to the learning. The memory of what is learned is not to be found in any specific brain region but rather in its unique cell firing rhythm. The brain's rhythms count for as much or more than the way it is put together.

—Daniel Goleman & E. Roy John, "How the Brain Works—A New Theory," *Psychology Today*

Thus, if your conscious mind is triggered by auditory signals (A), your subconscious mind to kinesthetic signals (K), and your unconscious mind to visual signals (V), this approach would call your thinking pattern AKV.

Each of these patterns reflects a natural flow of learning and self-expression, the give-and-take of experience as your system functions in balance. As an example, since my mind uses the VAK pattern, if I were to think about my friend Sam, I'd get a visual split-second flash of how he looked, what he wore, how his hair was cut, his name written on a letter. If I went a little deeper in my thoughts, I might remember the friendly words of a conversation we had and of saying to myself, "I really enjoy being with this man. He is so sincere. Sam is someone I can trust." Those words might trigger remote feelings of fullness in my chest, and if I stayed with them for a while, I could probably retrieve the feeling of his arm around my shoulders.

Thus, my brain uses all three symbolic languages to "think." As that thought is metabolized, visual recall is what comes first and seems most like conscious, organized "reality" to me. Auditory dialogue or verbal descriptions are right below the surface, in my subconscious thinking, and take a little longer to access. Feelings, touch, movement, and actions, although very profound, come from so deep in my unconscious mind that I do not usually "think" of them. My mind habitually tracks in this Visual-Auditory-Kinesthetic pattern.

Distinguishing Personality and Perception

It seems that at some point in our neurological development, the brain selects one specific pattern to sequence the conscious, subconscious, and unconscious channels, so that it can index experience efficiently. We all receive information on all three levels of thinking, but, as far as we know, it isn't possible, for example, for auditory input to trigger both heightened beta and alpha waves in the same brain. I have heard people swear that they know someone who is auditory in the front, middle, and back. That would make their pattern be AAA (auditory, auditory and auditory). You may even think you know one of those yourself. However, each of us, unless we are neurologically impaired, is affected by auditory information, visual information, and kinesthetic information. There's no way that you can escape input and impact from each.

These thinking patterns become as natural to us as being right- or left-handed. As natural as water is to a fish. Because they are in it all the time, fish don't even notice the water. The same is true for the patterns through which we filter our experience. Because they are so organic to us, usually we have no awareness of **how** we are perceiving the world, so we only think of our differences in terms of personality traits.

It's very important to understand that even though two people may have the same instrument, they may have very distinct person-

I learn through my hands and my eyes and my skin, what I can never learn through my brain.

—M.C. Richards, *Centering*

alities. Two violins can play very different music and still be violins. This is not about who you are—it's not a new kind of astrological sign. It's just how your mind processes information.

For example, Melissa and Peris both use the AVK pattern. They speak fluently, articulately, and frequently. Their idea of a good time is a long and detailed conversation about ideas and concepts. Neither one moves much during this conversation, and their eye contact is intermittent. If you observed them from the level of personality, however, all you would notice are differences. Peris loves to tell dirty jokes, speaks many foreign languages and seems very animated during conversation. Some people might call her an extrovert. Melissa on the other hand, is extremely serious, embarrassed at any mention of sex whatsoever, and speaks no foreign language. Most people would describe her as being a calm and aloof introvert. To find their similarities, you must recognize the similar ways they process their experience.

> The greatest enemy of any one of our truths may be the rest of our truths.
>
> —William James

What is the value of knowing your thinking pattern? Let's go back to the people I described in Chapter 2.

Remember Sally and her oppositional son? Their brains did process information in opposite ways—hers used the AVK pattern and his the KVA. But rather than disable him through labeling him as oppositional and in need of medication, she could realize that his need for movement and touch was not cruelty. His hitting the tree was merely his way of kinesthetically triggering his conscious mind. Perhaps that would give her an appreciation for how important touch really is to her son.

Or Jim and Susan, the couple who could not even go comfortably out on a date? Perhaps Susan's pattern was VAK and Jim's was KAV. It would be natural and habitual for him to touch casually or even to make love. For Susan, however, touch or making love would be a very profound experience, one that would not begin contact, but would be the ultimate form of intimacy. In the same way, Susan could come to understand that Jim's not looking at her didn't mean that he didn't love her. She could come to understand that his visual sensitivity was very similar to his kinesthetic sensitivity, and thus a bridge could be built between the two of them.

And Matt, our shop teacher and coach? His mind used the AKV pattern. If he understood this, one of the things he could do to help himself to study would be to walk around and talk into a tape recorder. And when he sits down to take a visually oriented test, he could close his eyes for a moment and remember the environment, the kinesthetic experience that he was having when he was studying the material. This would provoke his brain to access that material quite easily.

Joyce, our medical student? Since her mind used the KVA pattern, understanding that standing up in front of a group of people and delivering a speech could be a very challenging experience for anyone of that pattern might be the key to treating herself compassionately. This might open her to the possibility that using diagrams or a model to illustrate what it was she was going to say could make the words flow a great deal more easily.

I love this information, because it's empowering. You'll begin to realize how easy it can be to take charge of the times you space out and those when you don't; the process is as simple as standing up and moving around, or closing your eyes and rocking back and forth. Old ghosts of self-doubt and discouragement can be replaced by new awareness and self-appreciation.

Like fingerprints and voices, each person's learning style is different. It determines how students approach a task and remember information. It also shows what they know on a test.

—Lynn O'Brien, *NASSP Bulletin,* October, 1989

The Treasure Hunt: Following the Clues

I'm going to share several different ways of uncovering your pattern: a practice, an inventory, some portraits and descriptions of characteristics of each pattern, and some hints for communicating with each. Before we go any further though, how you go on this journey is as important as the destination you reach.

As you become curious about how your mind processes information, try to notice the whole pattern. Often times people will confuse themselves by considering only one specific characteristic and assuming that indicates what their pattern is. But it is the interrelationship and the sequence that's more important than any given characteristic.

Also, please do not expect yourself to fit any of the descriptions exact-

ly; no one does. Each pattern has a set of essential behaviors and qualities that most people with that pattern manifest fairly consistently, habitually, and comfortably, but we are *all* exceptions to the rules. There are wide variations among people of the same pattern—there are VAKs who are athletic, AKVs who read a lot, and VKAs who speak eloquently.

Another very essential thing to understand about your natural intelligence is that knowing how it processes information does not mean there is a limitation on what you can and cannot do. Anyone can do anything, in the same way that you can play any kind of music on any instrument. If, for instance, your theta consciousness is triggered by kinesthetic input, it does not mean that you don't enjoy sports. In fact, sports can be sacred to you. It also does not mean that you don't enjoy touch. It may mean that you don't enjoy **casual** touch. But touch can have a very profound effect on the unconscious mind, because it is being experienced in the most receptive state of consciousness.

Whether you've already figured out your pattern or simply have a mass of clues but no overall guess, I suggest that you use your mind much like a zoom lens as you continue this process. Go back and forth between paying attention to detailed behavior and taking in the whole of who you know yourself to be. Avoid zeroing in on one characteristic or one channel and making an assumption about a pattern.

Step back and be curious so your pattern becomes more or less of a nest rather than a pigeon hole, a way of connecting you with yourself and with other people rather than a way of putting each one of you in little boxes. Your uniqueness is, after all, your true abundance.

All paths lead to the same goal: to convey to others what we are. And we must pass through solitude and difficulty, isolation and silence, in order to reach forth to the enchanted place where we can dance our clumsy dance and sing our sorrowful song…

—Pablo Neruda

Practice: Discovering Your Pattern From the Inside Out

How do you discover *your* mind's pattern? You'll find clues to your pattern in your everyday life, in what you love or hate to do, in what's important or frustrating, in what's been a lifelong struggle. Did you hate gym class as a child? Do you need to see the big picture? Do you find it hard to stay awake while listening to a lecture? Can you walk and talk at the same time? What confuses you, what spaces you out or enlivens you, what makes it hard for you to concentrate, are all signposts of how your mind processes data.

Here's a practice to help you get started:

Notice how you think about something: not the content of your thoughts, but the process you use in thinking them. For example, if I ask you to think how many door knobs there are in your house, you might tell me, "Johnny Garcia built our house. He wanted to know whether we wanted hollow doors or louver doors. We had a disagreement over whether it would be possible to put a pocket door in that bathroom hallway . . ." That would be telling me the content of your thoughts.

If instead, however, you tell me that you became aware that when you think of how many doors there are in your house, you first see the hallways and feel as if you are walking through them, putting a hand on each knob, and then hear yourself counting, that would be noticing how you think about that memory. Noticing the process means noticing how you think about the content.

At first, noticing in this way may seem as awkward as holding a baby seems when you first try. Be patient with yourself, breathe and ease into it. Just notice the process you use to think about how many doors are in your house, and the sequence of symbolic language you use in that process.

The Personal Thinking Pattern Inventory

It can be tempting to pigeonhole ourselves and others. But this system exists precisely to help us move away from rigid notions of identity. So think of the inventory below as a guide—a map you can use to broaden your horizons and deepen your appreciation of yourself and others.

Mark the single answer to each question that most closely matches your experience. When you are finished, go back to see which pattern came up most frequently, and check that out with the descriptions of each pattern in the chapters that follow.

College students taught in the way they believed they learned, scored higher on tests of fact, knowledge, attitude, and efficiency than those taught in a manner dissonant from their orientation.

—George Domino, *ACT Research Report,* 1970

If no one pattern predominates, you may be influenced by unique variables beyond the parameters of this elementary inventory—or your pattern may be KVA, which tends to see itself in everything!

From what you can readily notice,

1. How would you describe how you talk?
- Words pour out confidently in logical order, without hesitation, using detailed vocabulary and a straightforward manner   AVK, AKV
- Shy or self-conscious about speaking in groups   VKA, KVA
- Use metaphors freely ("It's like a cyclone, a spinning top,") sometimes preceded by "Umm," or short hesitation VAK, KAV
- Make hand motions before speaking; must use hands or movements to find words   VKA, KAV
- Talk in circles; ask endless questions   VKA, KVA

2. How would you describe the way you make eye contact?
- Maintain steady, persistent eye contact   VKA, VAK
- "Eye shy"; look away frequently   AKV, KAV
- Eyes glaze over after lengthy listening   KVA, VAK

3. What do you remember most easily?
- What's been said; lyrics, people's names; memorize by just saying something repeatedly   AVK, AKV
- What's been seen or read; people's faces; memorize by writing something repeatedly   VKA, VAK
- What's been done or experienced; the feel or smell; memorize by doing something repeatedly   KAV, KVA

4. How would you describe your physical interaction with the world?
- Constantly and confidently in motion   KAV
- Can sit still easily for long periods of time   AVK, VAK

The voyage of discovery lies not in finding new landscapes, but in having new eyes.

—Marcel Proust

- Learning a physical activity can initially feel awkward, frustrating   AVK, VAK

- Learn physical tasks easily, by watching and doing with little or no verbal instruction   VKA, KVA

- High energy level, just beneath the surface   AKV, VKA

> I don't paint things.
> I paint the differences
> between things.
>
> —Henri Matisse

5. What is most likely to "space you out" or distract you?
- Too much visual detail; being questioned about the details of what you've seen   KAV, AKV

- Too many detailed words; being questioned about the details of what you've heard   VKA, KVA

- Too many options for activities; being questioned about what you feel in your body   AVK, VAK

6. What way of presenting information to a group would be the one in which you would feel the most self-confidence?
- Visual presentation (charts, photographs, slides, written information)   VAK, VKA

- Oral presentation   AVK, AKV

- Participatory activities   KVA, KAV

7. What do you remember most easily about someone you recently met?
- What you did with them or how you felt about them   KAV, KVA

- How they looked   VKA, VAK

- Their name or the conversation   AVK, AKV

8. What's most important when you decide which clothes to wear?
- How they feel; how comfortable you are in them   KAV, KVA

- The colors; how they look   VKA, VAK

- What they say about you; what calls to you   AVK, AKV

The Six Patterns: A Mental Topography

On pages 74–75 is a comparative chart of characteristics for quick reference. Each of the six patterns is then explored in depth in a chapter of its own to follow.

Practice: Move Over Ann Landers

*In 1988, a group of people, fondly known to us as the Madison Study Group, attempted to coerce me into teaching a session on how this perceptual approach could be used to enhance lovemaking. It was a blustery Saturday night in the winter wilds of Wisconsin. Wanting to warm things up a little, I agreed, IF **they** would first develop questions for a "Pamela Perceptual's Advice to the Lovelorn" column. What follows is the result of their efforts. You can check your mastery of perceptual patterns by deciding what thinking pattern is involved in each problem. If you learn better by "cheating," the answers follow. (The transcription of the requested lecture I delivered later that evening will be in the sequel to this book!)*

1. *Pamela Dearest,*
   I've got good grades, a sunny disposition, and a shining personality. The problem is I can't stop worrying about making a fool of myself. All I think about is my image, how I'll look to other people. I've been in therapy and my ego is shrunk down to the size of a pea, but I still am terrified of being seen. Any suggestions?
   Invisibly yours,
   E. Clipse

2. *Dear Pam,*
   Here's a new one for you. My business associate just bought himself earlids! I mean it! He puts them on whenever we're in a meeting together and I begin to talk. I don't have very much patience for people who

One way or another, if human evolution is to go on, we shall have to learn to enjoy life more thoroughly. Pay attention to what produces this kind (flow) of experience in your life and explore how to increase that.

—Mihaly Csikszentmihalyi, *Flow: The Psychology of Optimal Experience*

Category	AKV word smart, visually sensitive	AVK word smart, kinesthetically sensitive	KVA body smart, auditorily sensitive
Language Characteristics	Interacts easily by talking Has extensive vocabulary Speaks with lots of feeling and rhythm Likes telling others what to do (natural leader)	Interacts easily by talking Has extensive vocabulary Speaks logically about facts, ideas, concepts Likes having discussions about ideas	Typically soft-spoken Speaks concisely Rarely speaks in groups Needs silence to find words
Visual Characteristics	"Eye shy"—cannot maintain eye contact Sees whole picture Makes simple drawings Messy handwriting, unique style	Makes steady eye contact—may blink, flutter, or twitch Can attend to details and "big picture" simultaneously Can turn images around in mind Hard-to-read handwriting	Makes steady eye contact—may blink, flutter, or twitch Can attend to details and "big picture" simultaneously Can see images in mind from many angles
Physical Characteristics	Pent-up energy right below the surface Enjoys sports (good coaches, athletes) May initially be tentative about touch	May have sketchy sense of own body May be awkward, frustrated by physical activities—prefers free-form activities (running, swimming) to competitive sports Shy about touch, private about feelings	Interacts best by doing something together, physical contact Loves activity, moving, doing Likes to touch and be touched Typically well coordinated (natural athlete)
Learning Strengths & Challenges	Possible difficulty with reading, writing, spelling Can learn languages most easily by ear	Learns easily through discussion and lecture Can learn languages most easily by ear alone	Learns easily through hands-on, experiential techniques Can read well if taught experientially rather than phonetically
Typical Trouble	Interrupts others Can hurt others through sarcasm, wisecracking	Interrupts others Monopolizes conversations	Great difficulty expressing feelings in words
Frustrations	Hard to find satisfaction in turning visions into reality	Hard to learn physical skills without supplementary words or visuals	Many diverse interests (like drawing and ice hockey)
Natural Gifts	Visionary thinker Wants to inspire others	Great communicator Wants to help others understand	Wants to unite dissimilar elements
Famous People	John F. Kennedy, Julia Child, Adolf Hitler	Ronald Reagan, Barbra Streisand, Robin Williams	Benjamin Franklin, Toni Morrison, Albert Einstein

KAV body smart, visually sensitive	VAK visually smart, kinesthetically sensitive	VKA visually smart, auditorily sensitive	Category
Enjoys talking about personal experiences Likes telling stories Good at teaching activities, explaining movement Uses hands to find words	Speaks with feeling and emphasis Loves telling stories Talks out loud to sort ideas and make decisions	Speaks circularly from personal experience Uncomfortable speaking in groups Must move hands or body to speak	Language Characteristics
"Eye shy"—cannot maintain eye contact Can take in the whole of something at once Rarely aware of visual images Interacts best by doing things together, physical contact	Connects most easily with others through eye contact Face reveals feelings Likes visual order Can sit still for long periods	Connects most easily with others through eye contact Feels visual input Needs visual order to think clearly Pent-up energy right below the surface	Visual Characteristics
Constantly moving, doing Likes to touch and be touched Typically well coordinated (natural athlete)	May have sketchy sense of own body; needs to close eyes to feel May be awkward, frustrated by physical activities—prefers free-form activities (running, swimming) to competitive sports Shy about touch, private about feelings	Learns sports easily Has easy access to body sensations with eyes open Likes organized, competitive sports May get others' feelings and sensations confused with own	Physical Characteristics
Learns easily through hands-on, experiential techniques Can learn well through discussion	Learns well by reading and talking about or teaching others Difficulty with hands-on learning and structured, physical skill lessons	Learns easily by watching, then doing, without words or notes Difficulty with oral reading and reports, lectures, group discussion	Learning Strengths & Challenges
Difficulty finding positive outlets for energy	Shows off Can be overly helpful to make a good impression	May whine and complain Can go along with the crowd too much	Typical Trouble
Difficulty dealing with visually detailed information	Difficulty estimating how long something will take	Difficulty thinking independently	Frustrations
Wants actions to be useful to others	Great teacher—loves to show and tell Wants to illuminate	Great partner, collaborator Wants to create networks among people	Natural Gifts
Abraham Lincoln, Martina Navritilova, Clint Eastwood	George Bush, Jacqueline Onassis, Albert Schweitzer	Thomas Jefferson, Oprah Winfrey, Dalai Lama	Famous People

block us getting the job done, you know what I mean? I am great at assimilating information and figuring out exactly what needs to be done and then doing it or telling someone else to do it. Now what's wrong with that? I'll tell you—nothing! It's **him** that has the problem, right? Right!

Insulted,

Mike Crophone

3. Dear Pam,

My lover is addicted to an entity. I'm serious. She goes to this weirdo, who obviously is a multiple personality, and pays him a fortune to tell her what to do. Then she comes home and sounds like a tape recorder. I ask her what's for dinner, and she gets a blank look on her face and then says "The cosmic currents are directing us to eat wheatgrass." Is she possessed? He's ruining our lives, but she insists she's happier than ever and is about to move into their Center for Evolving Light. How do I get through?

Signed,

Bewitched, Bothered, and Bewildered

4. Dear Pamela,

I fall asleep when I read. Do you think I'm narcoleptic?? I get as far as the title of the book, and I'm gone. If I've just had a cup of coffee and read, I'm still gone—my mind spills right into the page. The next thing I know it's morning and I've finished the book but can't remember a word of what I read. This made school quite a challenge, but what's worse is I'm married to a writer who always wants me to read her stuff. She sent me erotic poems, and I read them before I went to sleep. The next afternoon, when I tried to bring the ones I liked best to mind, I couldn't remember a word of what I'd read.

One more thing—she hates how I dress. I don't get it. I like comfortable clothes, you know what I mean? She is always telling me I look like a slob, but if I dressed the way she wanted me to, I wouldn't be able to do a thing. What should we do? Please help, she's pouting and I'm in the dark.

Signed,

Blind Spot

5. *Dear Pamela,*

Uncle Lou and I just don't get along. I don't want to go home Thanksgiving, because he just sits for hours at the table and tells one joke after another. I can't get a word in edgewise. I want to throw a drumstick. I've tried to have some kind of connection with him, but he turns everything into an argument. He always wins—he learned all the tricks in law school. Help save our holiday.

Mute and Miserable

Pamela Responds:

1. Your pattern is most likely VAK, Ms. Eclipse, so what would help is learning to see **out** through your eyes instead of looking in at yourself as if through a hidden bank camera. Try taking a drawing class with nude models. Then get a large mirror, take off all your clothes, and do self-portraits. Learn to see yourself as a work of art. If your whole body seems too much, start with a foot, a finger, your left arm. When you are in a situation where you begin telling yourself you're making a fool out of yourself, get back behind your eyes. Whip out a little notebook if you have to, and start drawing whatever is around you at the moment.

2. There's a good chance your brain uses the AKV pattern, Mike. There's nothing wrong with you or him! Earlids for him are like eyelids for you. Here's a practice in compassionate understanding: at your next meeting, make yourself maintain eye contact with each person for as long as he or she is speaking—no sneaking little glances in the corners. Then you'll begin to understand what it's like for your associate.

Bring a handful of clay with you to the next meeting and work it with your hands when you begin to feel impatient, or get up and walk around. Close your eyes a lot. That will make it easier for you to listen. And do what you do well, offer your ideas. Don't be ashamed of your gifts. If what you want is harmony, though, you've got to listen as well. So play with your clay while you notice the effect your words have had.

Be a crazy dumb saint of your own mind... Have no fear or shame in the dignity of your experience, language and knowledge.

—Jack Kerouac

3. Your lover's mind probably uses the VKA pattern. Second possibility is KVA. Write to her about what you are feeling—write every place if necessary—the refrigerator, the toilet lid, tuck notes in her credit card bills, write your concerns on her belly in nail polish while she is asleep, on her back in massage oil while giving her a rub down. Don't *tell* her what to do! Write her how what she's doing affects you.

Life must be lived forward, but can only be understood backward.

—Søren Kierkegaard

4. I'd guess your mind uses the KAV pattern and your wife's uses the VAK pattern. Reading is a profound experience for you (as are art museums and even certain television shows and movies). Your eyes take in a drop and your mind expands it into a sea of visions.

Have your wife read selected sections out loud while you are giving her a foot massage or a back rub. Use your hands to describe how her poems make you feel. Explain to her that being able to determine how clothes feel on your body is as important to you as it would be for her to choose what she reads. Then teach her what makes for a comfortable feel for you. Let her experiment and buy you little gifts until she gets it right—hot pink silk boxer shorts, for instance!

5. Chances are, Uncle Lou's mind uses the AVK pattern and yours the KVA. That's why he can sit for so long, moving only his jaw-bones, and why your first impulse is to throw a drumstick in his face. Try a different approach. Go rub his shoulders. I guarantee it'll slow him down. If that feels just too personal, try playing cards. Or sketch the jokes he's telling into cartoons, or take notes, or walk backwards away from him while he's talking and grimace—all these things will help you connect at the common denominator you share: your visually triggered middle mind.

PERSONAL THINKING PATTERN CHAPTERS

Each of the patterns is presented in depth in the chapters that follow through snapshots, a description of characteristics, and a composite portrait, as well as guidelines for getting along and supporting. They are meant to help you use this tool in an artful way so you can trust the force of your own mind. It offers specific examples of people of each pattern so you can recognize the gifts and sensitivities of each.

The snapshots were developed over ten years, with input from thousands of workshop participants. The portraits were developed during a four-day seminar in Little Compton, Rhode Island by people who had been studying and teaching this approach for many years. The participants divided into perceptual pattern clubs, and spent several hours exploring commonalities and differences. Their discoveries were distilled into a personality and presented as a living portrait. Thus, each is a weaving of many aspects into one mythical representative—except for the KVAs. This group could only be comfortable if one person spoke for herself, describing just those aspects all had discovered they had in common.

CHAPTER 5

AVK:
AUDITORILY SMART,
VISUALLY CENTERED,
KINESTHETICALLY SENSITIVE

To laugh often and much; to win the respect of intelligent people and the affection of children; to earn the appreciation of honest criticism and endure the betrayal of false friends; to appreciate beauty and find the best in others; to leave the world a bit better whether by a healthy child, a garden patch, a redeemed social condition; to know even one life has breathed easier because you have lived—this is to have succeeded.
—Ralph Waldo Emerson (AVK)

> Our lives are like islands in the sea, or like trees in the forest, which co-mingle their roots in the darkness underground.
>
> —William James

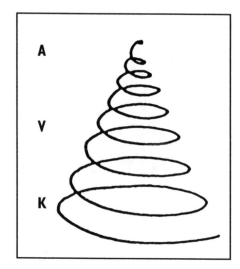

Easiest Way to Learn:
Hear/See/Experience

Easiest Way to Express:
Say/Show/Do

Pattern Snapshot

It's not hard to spot an AVK, because they can out-talk most of the people around them. Indeed, they are often considered "smart" because they can easily verbalize what they think and keep up with the pace of any conversation. Their words pour out in logical order without hesitation in a straightforward manner. They tend to speak in statements rather than questions. The content is largely conceptual, their vocabulary is relatively abstract and detailed; they tend to love facts, history, and ideas of all kinds. They are usually fascinated with language and can often learn to speak other tongues with ease. Music, the spoken word, humor, and puns are some of this pattern's delights.

AVKs enjoy explaining, debating, discussing, and arguing almost any idea. They are always trying to understand and want to help others do the same. They frequently use auditory vocabulary, with words and phrases like "hear, say, sounds, understand," or "That rings a bell," "Let's play it by ear," and "Talk to you soon."

AVKs get expressive when they talk, but their faces go flat when they move. They rarely use hand gestures when they speak; when they do, it will be for emphasis only. Although they can maintain steady eye contact, their eyes will blink, twitch, or flutter if they try to sustain it too long. They often need to look away to find their words, usually to the side.

People whose minds use this pattern are often shy about being touched and usually have a very sketchy sense of their bodies. They tend to perceive their body as a whole, so pinpointing and naming specific sensations can be very difficult. They are capable of ignoring bodily signals for long periods of time. About the only time they are speechless is when they are asked about their body sensations. In their learning pattern, there is not a direct link between words and feelings (A–K); they need a visual link in between. They have to get silent and create an inner visual image to bridge these two channels and access this information. Many times, instead of telling you how they feel, they will articulately express the reasons for their feelings.

> Better to be quarreling than lonesome.
>
> —Irish proverb

Composite Portrait: Amy Victoria Klemens

How do you do. Just call me Amy. I'm pleased to meet you. I organize parenting groups, as well as edit and publish a newsletter for parents and teachers. I'd like to tell you a little bit about my current life as well as my history, if you'll indulge me for just a few moments.

I teach women, mostly. But I'm also quite proficient at administering the entire network of parenting groups. I seem to be able to handle the day-to-day details of this job while simultaneously promulgating the overall vision of what we are all trying to accomplish. I used to run the local Weight Watchers groups, where I assisted women in understanding the whys and wherefores of their eating disorders.

My father is, was, I should say, an alcoholic, and my mother was sick for most of my adolescence. I have spent years trying to elicit some understanding out of this cacophony, but it is only recently, as I've begun to write about it, that the swirl of feelings that has plagued me is becoming clear.

I have been taking singing lessons for the last few years, but that is becoming boring. I'm much more interested in writing, drawing, and painting. I am quite proficient at entertaining people, and I do love to gossip. Sometimes I know I talk too much. Telling jokes comes naturally to me, too; perhaps that is the secret to my success.

If you want to treat me well, let me know you care by calling me up now and then and talking over difficulties between us if there are any. The worst thing you can do is to give me the silent treatment. Say what you mean and mean what you say. When we can exchange our individual truths, I know a real connection has been made. Please do not touch me until we know each other well. Thanks for listening.

I tore myself away from the safe comfort of certainties through my love for truth; and truth rewarded me.

—Simone de Beauvoir, *All Said and Done*

An Operator's Manual for Getting Along with AVKs:
Supporting Their Auditory Channel

What seems most important in talking with people whose minds use this pattern is to listen to them but don't fake it. Tell them if you can't listen and resume the discussion when you can. Let them know you are listening by responding specifically to what they've said. Refrain from making the same point over and over. Use words that are as precise as possible, and if possible give them verbal headlines first, e.g., "I'm going to talk about our contract." They can easily understand and enjoy subtleties of meaning. Realize that they grasp verbal instructions readily.

If they begin to argue with you, remember this is not serious for them, although it may be for you. If it is difficult for you, tell them as soon as possible that you'd rather stop and continue at some other time or in another form.

Supporting Their Visual Channel

People of this pattern often love to share visual activities: reading and discussing books and articles, especially ones that express differing viewpoints, playing card games, traveling and discussing what's been seen. Encourage them to write to themselves in a journal, or send you memos to allow their thinking to go deeper.

AVKs will need to look away to find their words; do not expect them to sustain eye contact for long periods of time.

Supporting Their Kinesthetic Channel

If your someone of this pattern is talking too fast or arguing relentlessly, suggest a kinesthetic or visual change to slow things down, help them go deeper, or alter the tone of the conversation: invite them to go for a walk with you or sit next to them instead of in front of them. Encourage them to draw a picture or diagram or use color to illustrate what's going on.

> He who knows that enough is enough will always have enough.
>
> —Lao-Tzu,
> *Tao Te Ching*

Placing your hand on their shoulder will also shift their verbal activity. You can also change the pace of things with a different kind of question. Ask them how they are feeling. They will have to get quiet to access this information; using kinesthetic vocabulary—action and feeling words—will slow them down.

People of this pattern need respect and understanding for their need to do and learn physical things in their own, sometimes slow-paced and private way. Follow their lead in doing physical activities together. Allow them to set the pace and the length of a walk, a swim, or a bike ride. Please don't insist that they do things exactly as you do. They may need privacy, space, and time to try things out on their own.

Avoid using physical humor, such as tickling, pranks, or practical jokes. Stay with verbal humor, where these people not only can hold their own, but shine.

CHAPTER 6

AKV:
AUDITORILY SMART,
KINESTHETICALLY CENTERED,
VISUALLY SENSITIVE

*Sound proves one of the major sources of
brain stimulus by which dynamic mental
vitality is maintained. Vocal sounds directly
resonate through the skull, chest, and body.
Our personally produced resonances can
charge and revitalize our body and brain.*

—Joseph Chilton Pearce (AKV)

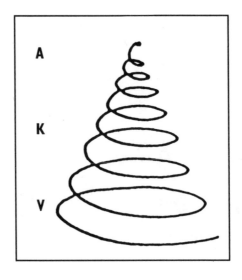

What the caterpillar calls the end of the world, the master calls a butterfly.

—Richard Bach,
Illusions

Easiest Way to Learn:
Hear/Experience/See

Easiest Way to Express:
Say/Do/Show

Pattern Snapshot:

The AKVs are both extremely articulate and have a high degree of physical energy right beneath the surface. They are natural leaders, love to take charge and tell everyone else what to do, discuss, argue, or debate anything, tell jokes, make plays on words. They understand and make verbal inferences easily and respond quickly to spoken questions, but can also wisecrack and be sarcastic. They usually have distinctive, one-of-a-kind voices, and speak clearly, precisely and with a lot of energy, feeling, and rhythm in their voice. More than anything, people of this pattern seem to want to inspire others.

AKVs will remember what is said to them and often can repeat what they've heard word for word, in tape-recorder fashion. This includes poetry, song lyrics, rhymes, and jokes. They often have strong feelings and opinions, which they express easily. Hand gestures usually follow their words and punctuate what they are expressing. AKVs can get their feelings hurt easily by what is said to them, but often don't realize the power of their words to wound others.

Listening may not be easy for people of this pattern. They may sometimes have the habit of interrupting others, especially if they are feeling a lot of excitement, unless they have been trained in debating or communication skills.

AKVs seem to have an endless supply of physical energy that is not easily released. While their bodies express how they feel, their faces rarely show it, and can look almost flat most of the time. They are sometimes eloquently coordinated and can easily learn physical moves if given verbal instructions. They generally like to participate in sports, but are even better coaches; they can easily find the words to teach someone else what to do.

AKVs get uncomfortable quickly if confined to a desk or small space for any length of time, especially if they are asked to deal with a lot of written material. Most of them are "eye-shy"—maintaining steady eye contact is very difficult, looking away or blinking frequently while talking is common. If they have trained themselves to maintain eye contact, they probably are still not seeing you.

People of this pattern are usually very particular about the visual images they choose—movies, television shows, and room decorations—since they are deeply influenced by what they see. A nasty look from someone else can make a lasting impression on them. AKVs will space out when they are given too much visual detail to look at, especially if it is not something they have chosen for themselves. Their eyes may also get distant when they are asked a question about what they see.

AKVs can be visionary dreamers. Many of them have vivid imaginations, which overflow with new ideas about how things could be. However, they may have trouble feeling satisfied when they can't quickly turn their ideas into reality.

> They always told me when I was young, "Just wait, and you'll see." Now I'm old and see nothing. It's wonderful.
>
> —Eric Satie

Composite Portrait: Arthur K. Vincent

How do you do. I am the originator of a form of psychotherapy that helps people integrate and embody their souls into moment-to-moment existence. My feelings are quite close to the surface, which used to be embarrassing for me when I was in the academic realm, where I was a molecular chemist, but is less so in the psychological. As long as I maintain my daily running practice and work out at the gym, I keep an equilibrium. Without that, I find myself overenergized. Physical activity seems to align disparate aspects of my life.

I've always felt a great deal of compassion for others in pain. I used to wrestle in college, and could feel my opponents falling on the mat when I threw them. I gave it up for debating, but I still enjoy many kinds of sports.

I adore music, play the guitar and sing, but I've never been really proficient at composing. I have been writing one poem about the natural world for three years. Writing is not easy for me. It is such a powerful experience that when I have written about something, I find myself living out what is on the page as if it were my map. Once I begin to write, I am one with the process. I lose awareness of anything else around me. But it does take me so long to get down to writing.

I have trained myself to look at people when I talk to them, but I am not comfortable doing it at all, and my eyes sometimes twitch as a result.

If you want to treat me well, bring as much of yourself as possible to the present moment of our experience, and tell me your truth. Be straightforward. Say what you feel and feel what you say. Understand that I am with you even when I look away or close my eyes. I would prefer to walk or at least stand as we talk, or do something while we are having a conversation.

> Whatever authority I may have rests solely on knowing how little I know.
>
> —Socrates

An Operator's Manual for Getting Along with AKVs:
Supporting Their Auditory Channel

What seems most important in talking to people whose minds use this pattern is to listen to them, discuss and appreciate their ideas. Let them know you are listening by asking them follow-up questions or commenting specifically on what you've found interesting in what they've told you. It helps AKVs listen better if you give them a one-sentence introduction to your conversation. For example, "I'd like to talk with you about how things are going in the lab." They appreciate clear, straightforward explanations, and love humor: use funny voices, accents, or jokes to get your point across, even in emotionally charged discussions.

These people have a finely tuned understanding of verbal language, but they tend to interrupt others or put words in your mouth. Let them know what the specific limits are around your availability. Tell them specifically when you will be off the phone or when you can give them your undivided attention.

Supporting Their Kinesthetic Channel

AKVs like to be in charge of what they do and how they do it. They organize by telling themselves or others what they are going to do. Music tends to have a mood-changing effect on them; listening to it or singing together can help them relax. Support their need for frequent outlets for their physical energy. Invite them to walk when you want to discuss emotional subjects. Talking about feelings will make them want to move, and moving will help them access their feelings in a more steady way. Walk with them in a side-by-side fashion, so they can look wherever they are comfortable. Touch will help AKVs settle down and get quiet. Avoid telling them how they feel; instead, tell them what you notice about their body language or tone of voice and ask them how they feel.

Supporting Their Visual Channel

AKVs tend to be inventors, idea people, systems thinkers. Encourage them to fully explore their visions, and inquire as to what they imagine it would take to realize those visions, and what kind of help might be needed.

If you write them a note or give them other visual input, make sure it is clear and simple. Allow people of this pattern to have control over their eyes. Don't require them to maintain eye contact or to look at anything that may be painful or uncomfortable for them. Disturbing visual images may replay in their minds for years.

> We need to recall that we do not make up or learn words in school, or ever have them fully in control. Words, like angels, are powers which have invisible power over us.
>
> —James Hillman

VAK:
VISUALLY SMART,
AUDITORILY CENTERED,
KINESTHETICALLY SENSITIVE

*To avoid being boring, I
often embellish my tales with color-
fully concocted extravagant elabora-
tions. By now, I believe whatever
I make up about myself.*
—Sheldon Kopp

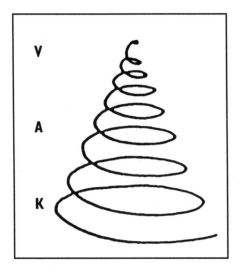

Eighty percent of life is just showing up.

—Woody Allen

Easiest Way to Learn:
See/Hear/Experience

Easiest Way to Express:
Show/Say/Do

Pattern Snapshot:

VAKs are recognizable as the people with bright eyes who could have invented "Show and Tell." More than anything, people of this pattern seem to want to help you see things in a new way. Many make a visual impression with the clothes they wear, which are usually chosen in colorful, well-coordinated outfits. They love visual details and *looking* at possibilities—flipping through catalogs, going window-shopping, or people-watching. They have the habit of devouring as much as possible of anything in print—cereal boxes, billboards, novels.

They are list makers, and generally like to take notes, though they may not need to go back and read them, because they memorize by reading, writing, and saying out loud what they need to learn. They can keep lots of details stored visually, sometimes to the point of having a photographic memory.

Since they have lots of feeling behind their words and you can usually see how they feel from the look on their faces, people of this pattern are often persuasive in their speaking. Hand gestures sometimes follow what they say if they want to emphasize a point. They like to teach and explain things, and love to tell stories in great detail, using lots of visual metaphors to paint pictures for their listeners.

When they speak, they tend to use visual vocabulary—words that present images—words like "see, look, colorful, show," and "bright," and phrases like "I can see your point," and "See you later." They often use fillers, like "um," "like," or "you know" between thoughts.

VAKs are often quite good at back and forth dialogue. They often find it useful to think out loud with someone else in order to decide between two options or to discover their own opinion about something.

VAKs' feelings are written all over their faces. In fact, you may know how they feel by looking at them before they are even aware of it. They light up when they speak, but their facial expressions go flat when they move.

Although VAKs maintain nearly constant eye contact while listening, they often will look up or to the side to think and find their words. They have to close their eyes to know how they feel in their bodies or what they want to do. When asked about their feelings, the pace of a VAK's language will slow down considerably. Some will be hesitant to speak at all unless they feel safe and comfortable with their questioner. You can often tell a lot about how they feel by the tone of their voice.

People of this pattern tend to have a sketchy sense of their bodies, may have to do a physical action over and over in order to learn it, and consequently often shy away from competitive sports. They can also be very private about their feelings; touch is not casual for them, so they are often hesitant to make physical contact. They may be aware of how their body feels as a whole, but it is very difficult for them to pinpoint sensations. They may know their leg hurts without being able to tell or show you the exact location of the pain.

VAKs can get impatient doing a repetitive activity. They will add their own variations rather than do the same thing in the same way over and over. For this reason, they may have trouble staying with the same task for a long period of time. To offset boredom, they will often go from one activity to another and then back to the first. They may change their minds frequently, even in the middle of something they've chosen to do. They sometimes have difficulty finishing tasks. This may be, in part, because they have a hard time estimating the

> The excursion is the same when you go looking for your sorrow as when you go looking for your joy.
>
> —Eudora Welty

amount of time it takes to do something.

VAKs get confused and space out when they are given too many choices of what to do, when they are asked questions about how they feel, how to do something, how they have done something, or when they are touched.

First, I do not sit down at my desk to put into verse something that is already clear in my mind. If it were clear in my mind, I should have no incentive or need to write about it....We do not write in order to be understood; we write in order to understand.

—C.Day Lewis (VAK), *The Poetic Image*

Composite Portrait: Veronica Alice Klinger

It's an interesting experience but quite difficult to have all of you looking at me. Saying that relaxes me a little. As does making myself see you. I usually like to talk with a table or a podium in front of me, but I looked around and didn't find one. I also get self-conscious without notes, because I imagine in my mind what all of you might say when you look at me.

I've always been involved with a lot of paper, and I've made many presentations based on my work. I'm much more comfortable with that. I've been asked to tell you what's the best way and the worst way to make love to me. That's much too personal. I think I'd rather talk about going to the movies instead. Some questions throw me off balance and leave me fumbling for words or cause me to say outrageous things that surprise even me.

I like to go to the movies a lot, but there are times I go too often. I consider myself a visual addict, because I sometimes choose movies or TV over the experience of real life.

Books are important to me. If someone comes into my house and reads the titles of my books and magazines, they know a lot about me right away. That's the part of me I want people to know. I have lots of books about lots of interesting things, many of which I've never read.

I tend to blame people in my mind, or myself if there's a problem. I see who's right, who's at fault, and then fiercely defend that picture of reality. That's what I do instead of going inside to really feel what's true in my body. I get a little righteous, well, I get **very** righteous, in order to keep myself from knowing how vulnerable I often feel.

I've decided to answer that question about making love to me, after all, at least in part. Before you learn that about me, we need to have many intimate conversations. You have to know me quite well, and be willing to hear me tell you about the things I do that nobody sees, and about my visions. You must show me you accept those things. Last year, I went ice skating on my frozen swimming pool in the winter to blasting music, all the while pretending I was in the Olympics! If those things are accepted, then we'll talk about making love!

An Operator's Manual for Getting Along with VAKs
Supporting Their Visual Channel

VAKs want most to be seen and heard, and to be appreciated for what they've read, what they've written, and what they've created visually. They love mail, both sending and receiving it. Send them letters, cards, and pictures; leave them little notes in surprising places. They get great pleasure from writing something that someone else will read.

Writing also helps people of this pattern bring their thinking into focus. If they seem confused about something, having a "paper conversation." can clarify things a great deal. If you want them to remember something, leave them a note. Giving them both written and verbal instructions may be most effective.

Understand that how things look is very important to VAKs. Tell them the effect that looking at them has on you. Eye contact is very important to VAKs. You know you have their attention when they're looking at you, but don't expect them to maintain it indefinitely—they need to look up and away while thinking; their eyes help them to find their words. Your facial expressions communicate a lot to them.

> The teaching that is written on paper is not the true teaching. Written teaching is a kind of food for your brain. Of course it is necessary to take some food for your brain, but it is more important to be yourself by practicing the right way of life.
>
> —Suzuki Roshi (VAK)
> *Zen Mind, Beginners Mind*

Supporting Their Auditory Channel

VAKs often need a lot of time to talk through the experiences of their lives: what they've done, how they feel, what they like, or what's hard for them. They may not fully know how they feel about anything until they talk about all sides of a given issue. They are curious about the patterns in their lives; using metaphor can help them explore these patterns in a creative, meaningful way. Often they don't want advice or agreement. They just want air time. Invite them to tell you what they are thinking and then listen.

> Those who justify themselves do not convince. To know truth one must get rid of knowledge; nothing is more powerful and creative than emptiness.
>
> —Lao-Tzu

People of this pattern love being interviewed, dialoguing back and forth, and helping others work through problems verbally. Sit face to face with them. Ask them expansive, curious questions. Tell them the effect their words are having on you. Be truthful, even about hard feelings. Explain things to them using metaphor and analogy. Be patient and *don't* interrupt when they tell you what they are feeling. Since this comes from a very deep place, their words will be slower, with more pauses. They may have to close their eyes or look up to find what they want to say.

Supporting Their Kinesthetic Channel

VAKs feel things deeply. Offer them quiet moments of just being with them as they tune in to their bodies and emotions. Allow them time to express what's going on, not only in words but in tears, laughter, or body movements. Please do not tell VAKs what they are feeling. If you notice an expression, tone of voice, or body posture that makes you curious, ask them about it.

Do things together at their rhythm, if possible. Please ask rather than tell them what to do. Avoid doing things for them. Give them clear time boundaries for accomplishing something and let them know the consequences of their not finishing on time.

Help them to break large tasks down into smaller, manageable parts. Make sure they include some variety or rotation in their expected responsibilities. They may not be consistent if they must stick to an invariable routine. Help them find phrases or pictures that will motivate them into action; place these motivators where they will see them often. Encourage them to give themselves visual and verbal acknowledgment for each accomplishment.

VKA:

VISUALLY SMART, KINESTHETICALLY CENTERED, AUDITORILY SENSITIVE

Sometime we shall have to stop overvaluing the word. We shall learn to realize that it is only one of many bridges that connect soul with the great continent of common life.

—Rainer Maria Rilke (VKA)

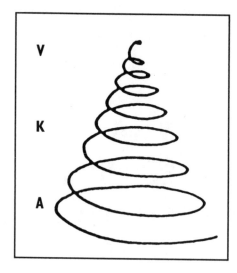

In a sacred manner they are sending voices.

—John G. Neihardt (VKA), *Black Elk Speaks*

Easiest Way to Learn: See/Experience/Hear

Easiest Way to Express: Show/Do/Say

Pattern Snapshot:

You may be struck right away by the empathetic energy of VKAs. They seem to drink in the world through their eyes and feel what they see. They are visually meticulous, wanting their clothes, possessions, and surroundings to fit an inner image they are trying to create. They can't think well with visual clutter. Most of them have legible handwriting, good spelling, and proofreading ability. Many like to draw and design things in detail. They tend to depend on written reminders, lists, instructions, and directions to keep themselves well organized.

VKAs connect with others most easily by making eye contact. They can often maintain it steadily, but their eyes glaze over if they are listening too long. They also tend to look up frequently when thinking and may have to close their eyes to listen in depth. The expressions on their faces seem to come alive when they move, but go flat when they speak.

VKAs remember most easily what they have seen or read. They will recall people's faces, but often not their names. People of this pattern have excellent eye-hand and eye-body coordination, learning best by watching a demonstration or reading the directions for a task and then experimenting in how to do it, *without being told first how to do it.* If they get stuck in the process, then they might ask questions and want some explanation. Some people of this pattern are voracious readers, while others have lifelong difficulty with reading, depending on how they are taught. Since the visual and auditory channels—the two modes involved in reading—are separated by the middle kinesthetic channel, unless a VKA's body, hands, feelings, or experiences are engaged in the process somehow, reading can be difficult. They may like to take copious notes in meetings. It is easy for them to write almost word for word what they hear. They memorize most easily by writing something repeatedly. People of this pattern are usually keenly interested in how things work, everything from complex machines to the human body.

Physical activity tends to be an important emotional and energetic outlet for them. They usually have a lot of wound-up physical energy just below the surface. People with this pattern are aware of the sensations in their bodies. Likewise, their feelings are often easily accessible to them. VKAs can also pick up the feelings and sensations being experienced by others they see around them.

They sometimes have a difficult time making decisions for themselves, as they often feel pulled in two directions and vacillate a lot before making up their minds. Experience seems to be their best teacher in sorting things out. If they can see and try out their options, they can often know what's right for them. VKAs are master collaborators, and much of their life seems to revolve around creating connections of one kind or another. They usually prefer to work in groups or on teams rather than independently. Their leadership style is often to maintain the connections between people.

At times, especially in large groups, they can be rather quiet and keep to themselves. It is difficult for them to speak off the top of their heads. There may be long pauses between their words or phrases when they speak, and they can get confused and space out when required to listen for long periods, or when asked questions about what they have heard.

At other times, with one or two peers, however, VKAs can be very talkative. They may jump from topic to topic repeatedly, making connections in their speaking that may not be understandable to

> This form of healing has nothing to do with books, and can't be learned from another person. It's a matter of feeling, having a fresh mind, knowing how to listen to what no one else listens to.
>
> —Dominanga Nancufil (VKA)

the listener, and that may never seem to get to the point. Gesturing, moving, or touching themselves helps them find their words. They may forget specific names or acronyms, but they are deep listeners, and highly sensitive to tone of voice and inflection.

People with this pattern use lots of visual vocabulary—words that paint images and phrases that include "look, see, show, imagine," "I can picture that," or "See you soon." They tend to ask endless questions that have no answers. If you attempt to answer them, frequently their response begins with "Yeah, but ..."

Composite Portrait: Vincent King Asner

I'm an architect. I can feel the way things could be when I look at them. I love designing exterior and interior spaces. I have a harder time when it comes to personal relationships. I guess I keep merging with the people I fall in love with—I get lost in them. My sister tells me I should see an analyst, because I am so afraid of long-term commitments. But the last one I saw kept telling me what I felt and what that meant and what I should do. At first I liked his certainty, but after a while I began sounding like him. It was as if his words came out of my mouth. I even talked in my sleep with the same accent he had! That was going too far. Back to the drawing board for me.

I hate verbal fights and arguments. I pull as far away as I can in my mind. I've been accused of not remembering what people say, but that's not true. My brain can be like a tape recorder. Especially for words that carry a lot of feelings. But sometimes I do have a tendency to remember words in a "creative" way.

If it's quiet around me, I can see what I need. If I want to really hear something, I need to close my eyes. I tend to daydream my way through decisions, and then, in my own time, carry them out. Afterwards, I can explain to myself and others what I've done. I don't like to be told what to do. Well, that's not exactly true; **part** of me likes rules and structure, and a secret part hates them. I try very hard to do what I'm supposed to, but there is a hidden part of me that yearns to be BAD! I always seem to be searching for my true identity.

I feel what I see. Have I said that? I can almost always tell what

To begin writing from our pain eventually engenders compassion for our small and groping lives. Out of this broken state there comes a tenderness for the cement below our feet, the dried grass cracking in a terrible wind. We can touch the things around us we once thought ugly and see their special detail, the peeling paint and gray of shadows as they are— simply what they are: not bad, juts part of the life around us—and love this life because it is ours and in the moment there is nothing better.

—Natalie Goldberg, *Writing Down the Bones*

others are feeling, but it is sometimes hard for me to differentiate between what I imagine they are feeling and what I intuit. Walking makes it easier for me to talk. Words don't come easily to me. When I make love, I like silence or music with no words. When I hear words, I **have** to listen to them.

If you want to treat me well, make eye contact with me, and do something with me. Last come the words, soft words. Don't say one thing and do another.

> The power of memories and expectations is such that for most human beings the past and the future are not as real, but more real than the present.
>
> —Alan Watts

An Operator's Manual for Getting Along with VKAs
Supporting Their Visual Channel

Writing may be a more effective way of communicating with VKAs than speaking. They will be able to grasp more easily what you are trying to convey than if you say it to them. Encourage them to write as well. This will allow their thoughts to come into focus and help them communicate more succinctly with less spiraling. When they read what they have written, it helps them find the cohesive meaning in what they are thinking. Writing is also an effective way for them to express the many feelings they have inside.

In conversations with VKAs, give them as much eye contact as possible. Write down what they say for them so they can refer to it later. Otherwise what they have said may seem to evaporate in their mind. Encourage them to take notes during phone conversations or in any other important verbal communication. Also, write down the questions they are currently wondering about. This will help them think for themselves as they live out the answers.

VKAs will know that you care for them most clearly from letters, notes, cards, or other visual remembrances, such as gifts or flowers.

Supporting Their Kinesthetic Channel

In being so aware of how others feel, VKAs can easily lose their sense of themselves. Because of this, it is essential for them to learn to recognize their own body signals and emotions as distinct from everyone else's. Otherwise, in order to protect themselves from feeling too much from others, they may learn to shut down their awareness of sensation altogether and not be in touch with their own bodies.

Encourage them to take the time to discover how they feel. Frequently turn their attention to themselves with questions like: What is this like for you? Suggest they move or take physical space in order to find their answers.

As strange as it sounds, suggest that they talk with themselves in the mirror to discover what they want and think. When they are looking only at themselves, they can feel their own feelings better than when they are around other people. Solitude will help them when they feel pulled in two directions at the same time.

Life is far too important a thing ever to talk about.

—Oscar Wilde

Supporting Their Auditory Channel

VKAs are easily influenced by what they are told about themselves. Make sure that your words and tone of voice support their positive self-esteem. What you say to them will go in very deeply. Whenever possible, criticism should be written, not spoken. Avoid using sarcasm with people of this pattern. Their auditory channel is very literal. They will take in the biting tone of voice and may not understand at all what you say.

It is vital for people whose minds work in this way to feel heard. Allow them time to speak; have patience with their spiraling words. Really listen and mirror back to them in words or in writing what they have said.

VKAs need to ask a lot of questions. You don't need to answer them. Instead, direct their attention back to themselves—their own words, experiences, or viewpoints. Allow time for silence and for pauses in the midst of conversations—do not finish their sentences, interrupt them, or put words in their mouths.

It is often more effective to ask them, "How do you feel about...?" rather than "What do you think about...?" It will help them stay more present to focus on feelings. Asking their opinion can cause them to space out. Pay attention to when VKAs' eyes glaze over. You may be talking too fast, too intensely, or too abstractly.

CHAPTER 9

KVA:

KINESTHETICALLY SMART,
VISUALLY CENTERED,
AUDITORILY SENSITIVE

*Why am I interested in both the physical world
of handcrafts and agriculture and in the world of psyche and
eros? Why does the archetype of wholeness speak so strongly
despite a society where specialization and prejudice are tout-
ed? Why did I start out wanting to be a student of ancient
Chinese language and history, a culture in which writing was
a form of painting, and in which language was valued both
for its poetic feeling and for its artistic form in calligraphy?
Why do I feel the mystery of the world so strongly, as a
sacred presence, in nonverbal as well as verbal forms—in
poets as well as poems? Why do I keep asking why?*

—M.C. Richards

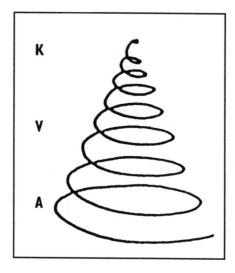

Easiest Way to Learn:
Experience/See/Hear

Easiest Way to Express:
Do/Show/Say

The words or the language as they are written or spoken, do not seem to play any role in my mechanism of thought. The psychical entities which seem to serve as elements in thought are certain signs and more or less clear images which can be voluntarily reproduced and combined. The above mentioned elements are in my case of visual and muscular type. Conventional words or other signs have to be sought for laboriously…

—Albert Einstein (KVA), as quoted by John Briggs, *Fire in the Crucible*

Pattern Snapshot:

People whose minds use the KVA pattern are private with a grounded physical presence and seem to be surrounded by a deep silence. They have smooth, receptive energy and seem to be most alive when they are moving. They often are interested in seemingly diverse and dissimilar things—football and art, for instance, or sewing and chemistry. They seem to have an intuitive sense of how it all fits together. Their life often is about living from a place of integrity.

KVAs like to be "doing" as much as possible; they tend to be concrete learners, and can acquire new physical skills with ease by doing and watching and only occasionally asking questions. They are very well organized and detailed in what they do, and diligent workers when they believe that they can succeed. They generally have good eye-hand coordination, often like working with their hands, and are easily able to put things together, sometimes in very creative ways.

KVAs are generally very aware of the specific sensations in their bodies. Since physical comfort is quite important to them, they may go to great lengths to find the right chair or the right position to sit in. They tend to choose clothes that are comfortable and allow freedom of movement, with some awareness of how they look.

People of this pattern feel things deeply, but it may be almost impossible for them to express their emotions in words. They can become sullen and stubborn if they feel someone important to them is not on their side. When they are angry they tend to withdraw rather than lash out. Touch usually comes naturally and easily to them (unless they have been trained out of it), and they need both to touch and to be touched.

KVAs tend to choose to be alone or with one or two others rather than be a part of a large social gathering. If they are in a group, they will often look for a quiet place to sit back, watch, and listen. They tend to be soft-spoken people who enjoy working or playing alone or with one special friend, and often find it easier to relate to animals or nature than to people.

People of this pattern can maintain steady eye contact, but their eyes blink, twitch, or flutter if they try to sustain it too long. Their eyes will glaze over if they listen to too many words, and they usually need to look away to the side to find what they want to say. Their facial expressions usually go flat when they speak.

KVAs have a three-dimensional way of making images. This means that, literally and figuratively, they see things from many perspectives. They can turn letters, words, pictures, designs, and diagrams around in their minds. They can also see the validity of many sides of an issue and the whole of something as well its details.

It may be especially difficult for people of this pattern to talk about feelings, since the kinesthetically triggered conscious mind and auditorily triggered unconscious mind are separated. KVAs can become overwhelmed easily by having to listen to too many words. They may get overwhelmed easily by a lot of words and space out if they have to sit still, look intently at something, and listen, because the unconscious part of their mind is being triggered. This also means that they are affected deeply by what is said to them. Harsh or critical phrases can echo in their minds for years. Whenever possible, criticism should be written, not spoken. People of this pattern need to feel safe, accepted, and listened to in order to enter deeply into conversations—which is the only way conversations really happen for them. Casual chitchat is awkward and difficult. Speaking in

> Only when one is connected to one's own core is one connected to others. And, for me, the core, the inner spring, can best be refound through solitude.
>
> —Anne Morrow Lindbergh (KVA), *Gift From the Sea*

front of groups can also be difficult unless they have visuals or hands-on cues to bridge the gap. They don't like to talk off the top of their heads, and may freeze if pressured to speak.

There may be frequent pauses in a KVA's speech. They frequently take a long time to answer a question, find the name of something, or the word they're looking for. Their answers may be short, concise, and sometimes surprisingly unique and insightful. Their responses may be circular, sometimes never getting to the point. Their greatest gift can be in the quality of their listening and in the depth and breadth of the questions they ask, questions that often cannot be answered.

People of this pattern frequently use a lot of kinesthetic vocabulary, words that convey action or feelings, like "grab," "hold," "soft," or "move," and phrases like "That feels right," or "I'll be in touch soon."

[Albert Einstein] had a serious speech problem which some have claimed (probably incorrectly) was dyslexia. He constantly repeated things to himself and seemed headed for the label retarded. But his mother introduced him to music, which acted as a psychological safety valve. He began to sing to himself, and was much more coherent when he sang than when he spoke. If he was asked what he was singing, he would say, I'm making up songs for God.

—John Briggs,
Fire In the Crucible

Composite Portrait: Karen Vivian Appleton

Being true to myself is most important. People say I keep a lot hidden, but that's not really how it is. If I don't feel safe, I make myself invisible by blending in with the background.

Moving helps me think and be comfortable—you might say I like to wonder and wander. I find that making eye contact for too long is distracting. So I pace or jiggle, looking now and then to touch base and see if others are paying attention to me.

I love to envision possibilities, imagine all the different ways something would look, see things from every perspective. My images often are three dimensional. If I imagine I'm in a certain place, it's just like being there. If I make images as if I'm looking in on myself, however, I can't speak at all.

Which is one of my problems. Speaking to people casually, that is. Starting to speak feels like jumping off of a high bridge. It's important to me too, because I just have to say something to somebody who will listen without interrupting or putting words in my mouth, so I can see if it's really how I feel.

Mostly I need to know that I'm being heard. The silence that's around me tells me my words have been received, which is very important to me because if my words aren't received, I shut down, withhold, and don't want to extend any more. I'll go away or get snippy in order to get your attention back.

I seem to be a perpetual student of things; I'm always in the school of life. I used to feel I was dumb, particularly when it came to verbal tasks, although inside I knew that wasn't true. I was always looking out the window. I loved gym and lab sciences. If I couldn't be learning in a concrete way, I'd lose interest and think about other things. I've found talking to someone after I've read something helps me. I need to get up and move around frequently, then write what I'm reading back to myself.

People tell me I'm very innovative. Maybe, but sometimes I think of myself as a loner. Nature is my church, where I feel most whole. In relationships, I tend to be like a wave, moving in and moving out with my own tides.

I feel loved and well-treated if I'm touched with hands that are feeling. I hate being told I look like someone else. I hate when someone finishes my sentences for me. I also don't like it when people say words that aren't really what they mean. I don't know what I'll say until I say it. I don't know what I've said until I hear it.

> You've got to have something to eat and a little love in your life before you can hold still for anybody's sermon on how to behave.
>
> —Billie Holiday (KVA)

An Operator's Manual for Getting Along with KVAs
Supporting Their Kinesthetic Channel

People whose minds use this pattern want to be joined in activity and adventure, and to be appreciated for what they know how to do. The most effective connections begin with doing something together, as much as possible, out in nature with them. This is where their natural leadership style comes out—they love to be followed in action. They need to see that their efforts have contributed.

If a KVA withdraws when his or her feelings are hurt, give some space. Don't prod verbally. A gentle touch may be the best way to help reconnect when he or she is ready. It is often more essential to them that they can go at their own rhythm than that they reach a particular destination.

Supporting Their Visual Channel

It is very effective to use the visual channel to communicate with KVAs so they can have a breather from talking and listening: write them notes. Encourage any budding interest they may have in the arts, photography, drawing, sculpture, weaving, woodworking. This may give them a nonverbal way of expressing how they feel.

Find activities that involve looking at something together: pictures they've drawn, a favorite TV program, a sporting event, a movie, card games.

Supporting Their Auditory Channel

Above all, have patience with KVAs' silence and their need for it. Allow them to come to you with questions and statements. Prodding them to talk can make them retreat further into themselves.

Avoid chitchat or small talk. Invite them to tell you about their experiences—they will talk more comfortably about what they've done than about how they feel. If you ask them a question, allow them some silent time to think. Don't tell them what they think or finish their sentences. Listen all the way through, even if you think you know what they are going to say. They may surprise you.

People of this pattern navigate through their lives by asking endless questions, looking for possibilities, and living out the answers. No matter how much you are tempted, do not answer these questions. Bring their attention back to themselves. Sometimes just being silent is the best way to do that—or answer with an honest "I don't know."

Create conversational environments where KVAs can look wherever they want, preferably in nature. Encourage them to take notes or move or play with something while conversing. Provide actual or mental pictures or concrete examples when explaining a new or abstract concept.

Be truthful and literal when speaking with them. Don't exagger-

Words cannot always be trusted. Words mean too many things to different people. If I listen with my feelings, then I understand what others really know about life. If I listen without my feelings, then I understand what others know about things. I do not think they remember how to listen to feelings…

Most of my teachers and friends do not remember that words alone are not enough. So I do not trust the way others hear my thoughts. I can listen to their words and their hearts, but they do not understand my language. I think I'll be quiet until I can be heard without words. It's easier to communicate by drumming and singing.

—An eighth grade Liberian student, quoted in *The Roar of Silence: Healing Powers of Breath, Tone and Music*, by Don G. Campbell

ate unless you make it clear that you are. Be aware that they are very sensitive to negative tone of voice as well as words. What you say to them, and how you say it, will go in deeply.

Listening to KVAs' favorite music with them can be a powerful and intimate way to connect.

CHAPTER 10

KAV:
KINESTHETICALLY SMART,
AUDITORILY CENTERED,
VISUALLY SENSITIVE

(When asked if he ever felt fear:)
I feel what you feel. You name it fear.
I name it a call to action.

—Morehei Ueshiba,
the founder of Aikido

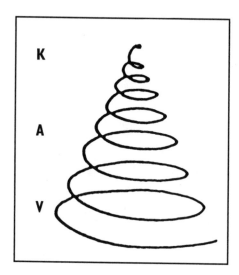

> Individual minds are connected to a universal mind. All people need to do is find out how to get it and reach it when they need it. Karma is simple truth: you reap what you sow.
>
> —Willie Nelson (KAV)

Easiest Way to Learn:
Experience/Hear/See

Easiest Way to Express:
Do/Say/Show

Pattern Snapshot:

You'll recognize people with the KAV pattern by how present they seem in their active bodies and their shy, sensitive eyes. They seem to be constantly in motion. Even when sitting, they are rarely still. Their preference is to relate to the world first in some tangible way—by touching, tasting, smelling, or experiencing anything new with their hands or their whole bodies. They tend to be well-coordinated, "natural" athletes who like competitive sports, seem to have an endless supply of physical energy.

KAVs learn things that involve the use of their bodies very easily and their movements are strong, steady, direct, and detailed. They like to work with their hands, tinkering with cars, working with wood or crafts. They are competent "doers," preferring to be on their feet and in action rather than sitting at a desk. They generally have amazing physical stamina and do things in a logical fashion, which they may take for granted.

People with this pattern are able to access and verbalize body sensations in a specific, organized way. They can tell you exactly where their head hurts or which muscle in their leg is pulled, or precisely where they want you to scratch their back. Physical comfort is quite important to them. They may go to great lengths to find the right chair, the right position to sit in, or to choose the clothes that have just the right weight and texture.

Touch comes naturally and easily to most KAVs; it is a casual but important way to connect. They need both to touch and to be touched. In general, these people are keenly aware of their emotions. But you won't see how they feel on their faces. KAVs generally have flat facial expressions; their bodies speak for them in how they stand, move, or touch.

KAVs' hand gestures will often precede a spoken thought, as though the movement helps them conduct the words out, like a maestro's baton. They enjoy talking about what they have been doing, how they did it, and how it felt to do it. They tend to get bored easily with discussing abstract ideas. They are, however, very effective at talking about taking action, using a lot of kinesthetic vocabulary—words and phrases that describe action or feeling, such as "getting a feel for," "How does that grab you?," or "I can't get a handle on it." They might end a conversation with "Catch you later," or "Let's get together soon." They frequently use kinesthetic metaphors when they speak: "Throw it fast and fierce like a bullet."

KAVs are especially skilled at teaching people how to do things since translating action into words is easy for them. They often want to convince others to do things their way.

Sometimes KAVs need to sort things out loud. They may start a conversation talking about the different choices they have, but by the end, they will know which option will work best for them as a result of having talked it through.

KAVs prefer to keep their eyes averted, making occasional glances to check in with the person speaking. If required to "look" for too long, their eyes may seem distant or glazed over. They can listen intently, making little or no eye contact at all, even while busy doing something else. Many KAVs act timid or tough if they are being looked at, particularly by strangers in public.

People of this pattern are deeply influenced by external visual images. Nasty looks, ones that indicate judgment or criticism, can be more painful to them than even physical or verbal punishments. Even the way food looks on a plate can be offensive to them. Smiles

Sometimes the skin seems to be the best listener, as it prickles and thrills, say to a sound or a silence; or the fantasy, the imagination: how it bursts into inner pictures as it listens and then responds by pressing its language, its forms, into the listening clay.

—M.C. Richards,
Centering

Our minds want clothes as much as our bodies.

—Samuel Butler

and looks of love and appreciation can likewise leave a lasting impression. Notes, cards, or pictures that are written or drawn for them can also affect them for a long time.

KAVs are often reluctant readers; their eyes have difficulty focusing on the details of tiny, closely spaced print. Thus, they tend to read infrequently, but when and if they do, they can get totally immersed in it, remembering most easily what happened or how the characters felt in what they read.

Writing can be a laborious task for people of this pattern, and it can also be their art form, if they can do it at their own rhythm without too much criticism. KAVs can be easily overwhelmed by too much visually detailed paper. Their preference is to take in a wide view, the "bigger picture"; they can capture the whole of something with just a quick glance. Consequently, they are also expert "finders," able to locate a needle in an entire haystack.

Portrait: Andy Bryner, A House Divided

I loved learning when I was a little kid. I went to work with my dad in the Pennsylvania oil fields. As we drove through the woods in a Jeep, I'd ask millions of questions. He taught me about geology, dinosaurs, rock strata, and electricity, patiently explaining and drawing. He built a little work space for me, a tool house in the woods, where I played by imitating him.

When I went to school, the emphasis in my life shifted to fitting in, getting good grades. I tried to please everyone, but my body suddenly seemed to be in opposition to my mind—I felt split. The teacher was always telling me to sit still. But if I didn't jiggle, I felt like the world was closing in on me, like I was in prison.

As I got older, I learned that what was most important to me, my feelings, were supposed to be kept quiet and controlled. What I loved—mountaineering, sports, using my hands—was for the "Shop Kids," the jocks. If I pursued those, I'd never get anywhere. So I got straight A's, looked good on the outside, but became increasingly unhappy inside. Good grades, then a good job, the right contacts, the right image. I learned to survive and to look good by faking it.

Inside I knew I was pretending. Outside no one cared. All through college, marriage, a banking job in Manhattan, an MBA program, a part of myself was dying. In the pain of pretending, I became more and more addicted to "back doors": affairs, alcohol, drugs, any way I could sneak some stolen moments, secret rewards, to numb the pain and control what I felt. My energy vacillated between outbursts of anger and not caring any more. My mind was divided between secret passions and strategies.

At the time of the killings at Kent State, I reached a crisis point. My spirit was internally hemorrhaging. I dropped out of the MBA program, got a divorce, and became an apprentice carpenter. After a time, I switched from working with wood to working with people as a massage therapist and then a chiropractic assistant. With Dawna's support, I began to learn the pattern of my mind, and became re-acquainted with my feelings. I came to honor the way my mind works.

I had wanted to touch people my whole life, yet where I grew up, bodies and touch were treated as dirty, secret, unimportant, forbidden. But through her work, for the first time since I was six, I knew I was on a path. I came to understand what I was doing with all of my energy. My mind was alive as it had never been in school. I followed **its** way—experience first with hands on, then discussions, then books. I learned anatomy, physiology, nutrition quickly, because it was presented in a language my mind could understand. I didn't have to try, or use will power to apply myself, it was all natural. I came to understand that I had always wanted to touch, to move, to do, because that's what my brain needed so it could process information. Feelings were so important to me because they were my native language. There was nothing wrong with me! I was **not** schizophrenic, perverted, or too sensitive!

I also came to understand the allegiance I had always felt to farmers, laborers, carpenters, waitresses, and many others who seemed to be lost in the shuffle, believing they could never get anywhere. I came to understand the compassion I had always felt for those who felt trapped in laboring jobs, the army or prisons, and, often, addiction.

Schools actually penalize kinesthetic learners and reward auditory and visual. Research verifies that beginning readers and poor readers tend to be strongly kinesthetic.

—Marie Carbo
& Rita Dunn

I feel lucky. I understand now that it's possible to be whole, to have my body, mind, and passion under the same roof, in a house that doesn't need back doors, where 35 years of pain and anger at pretending can finally come to rest.

The creative spirit creates with whatever materials are present. With food, with children, with building blocks, with speech, with thoughts, with pigment, with an umbrella, a wineglass, or a torch. We are not craftsmen only during studio hours. Any more than man is wise only in his library. Or devout only in church. The material is not the sign of the creative feeling for life: of the warmth and sympathy and reverence which foster being; techniques are not the sign. The sign is the light that dwells within the act, whatever its nature or medium.

—M.C.Richards,
Centering

An Operator's Manual for Getting Along with KAVs
Supporting Their Kinesthetic Channel

You can connect well with people of this pattern by doing activities together, being physically affectionate, and letting them know you appreciate what they do and how well they do it.

Exchange new ways of doing things. Don't insist that they sit still. Keep in mind that moving, and fidgeting help them to stay alert. Also keep in mind that being of use is what their life is all about.

Respect a KAV's need to be physically comfortable. They will be easily distracted by clothes that don't fit well or that irritate their skin. Understand that they may have to adjust their position continually to maintain comfort. They may be very particular about bedding, furniture, and the feel of their sports equipment.

People of this pattern may act first and speak later. If you are frightened by their abrupt movements or actions, or if they tend to act out what they are feeling instead of speaking about it, encourage them to walk with you or do something physical—hitting softballs, throwing rocks in a river—and then wait and listen for the words that will come. They prefer that you be very explicit about your boundaries of what behavior is and is not acceptable.

Supporting Their Auditory Channel

Invite KAVs to talk about their feelings and their personal experience. Instead of asking, "What are you thinking?", try "What are you feeling?" or "What have you been doing?"

Talk while doing something: walking, playing basketball, or cooking dinner. Having something to hold and play with in their hands may also help KAVs pay attention, as will physical proximity and standing or sitting side by side instead of face to face. As much as possible, speak to them in action or feeling words; explain things in terms of how to do something, how it works, or how it might feel.

Allow time for them to sort things out loud when they are confused. It's important for them to talk through and evaluate what they hear and to learn to speak what's true for them. Music can have a powerful effect on the emotional and physical state of people of this pattern. Soothing songs or instrumental music may be effective in helping them settle down or ease into sleep. They can also find singing and playing music satisfying—as an outlet for both their creative self-expression and their physical energy.

> Millions of persons long for immortality, who do not know what to do with themselves on a rainy afternoon.
>
> —Source unknown

Supporting Their Visual Channel

KAVs have minds that can see the whole of a situation in a glance and observe solutions from a wide perspective; at the same time, they find it difficult to notice visual details. For example, they can look at someone and tell you what that person is feeling without noticing the color of his or her eyes or what he or she is wearing.

Ask them about their dreams and their imaginings. Talk with them about a step-by-step action plan that will make it possible to convert a vision or picture into reality. Respect the sensitivity of their visual channel. Don't tell them what to look at or what they did or did not see. Honor their decisions to hide their eyes or move away from visual images that may be painful or uncomfortable for them. Both pleasant and unpleasant "pictures" can stay in their minds for a long time.

CHAPTER 11

COMING HOME TO YOURSELF

The majority of people are subjective
toward themselves and objective toward all
others, terribly objective sometimes, but the
real task is, in fact, to be objective towards
oneself and subjective towards all others.
—Søren Kierkegaard

This chapter illustrates the use of personal thinking patterns to get unstuck in your thinking, to relate to the "same old problems" in new ways. Through an empirical practice, and stories of how people of each pattern have used this approach, you are offered deeper ways of implementing this information in your life.

A mind that is stretched to a new idea never returns to its original dimension.

—Oliver Wendell Holmes

Most adults move through a learning experience by asking themselves three questions. Each one serves as a gate which, depending on the response, determines whether it will open to the next stage of the journey. They are: **"What** (is this about?)," **"So What** (How is this relevant to me?"), and **"Now what** (How can I use this in my life?)."

On the morning of the second day of workshops where we teach this information, people usually come into the room with their minds full of "Now what?" type questions. Often, the first ones they ask are about other people, about the "theys" in their lives instead of the "I's": "What do you suggest so that my Aunt Mary understands that Uncle Sylvester's brain uses a KAV pattern and that's why...?"

We always ask people to bring this learning home first, to use it as a tool to relate to themselves, before using it to relate to others. Since this chapter is filled with stories about how other people do that, I'd like to invite you to experience the movement of your own mind through the spiral as an entry point to the rest of the chapter.

The practice that follows was inspired by Aldous Huxley. He used to call it "deep reflection," and did it for five or ten minutes when he was stuck trying to work through some snag in the fabric of his thought. It seems to help the mind balance itself, and shift to a focus on where you are free rather than where you are stuck.

Knowing Empirically: Rafting in the River of Your Mind

- *Begin by redirecting your attention from whatever it is stuck on to an awareness of the external world: Shift to perceiving just what is through the symbolic language of your conscious mind for a few moments. (In my case that would be to what I see). As you inhale, experience the way your eyes or ears or skin are absorbing what you perceive.*

- *Now shift back perceiving the world through the symbolic language of your subconscious mind (I become aware of the sounds around me, the rustling of papers in the wind ...)*

- *Slowly slip into an increased awareness through the unconscious mode (I'm floating in the feelings of my breath, moving in and out, the smell of nutmeg ...)*

- *At some point, your mind may begin to "wander wider" off into images—visions, songs, feelings, ideas. (... which reminds me of the first time I tasted eggnog with Adrienne Fisher on New Year's Eve when I was 12.) Give yourself permission to just follow your mind wherever it goes for a few moments.*

- *When you are ready to notice externally again, bring yourself into concentration again by reversing the process, increasing your awareness of the mode that triggers your subconscious mind, then your conscious mind, as it brings you fully alert to the moment.*

    For just a moment, pay attention to how you were affected by all of that. Whether it was hard or easy, unfamiliar or delicious, is not as important as how it affected your rhythm, clarity, sense of balance.

Some people who are very adept at controlling their lives in a set way find this practice quite challenging. To allow one's mind to **be** shaped by present experience can be as awkward at first as riding a bicycle without training wheels. But since this practice is natural to your mind, just as balancing is, you will probably find that within a very short time reality will be a delightful ride.

Knowing Metaphorically

In Hawaii, it is common for people to "talkstory." As you sit down on a wicker chair on someone's front porch, they are apt to begin telling you how they came to make that chair and how their grandfather taught them to weave in that particular way with plants that grow behind the house in the nearby mountains. The weaving of stories that unfolds is also a means of enfolding you into a much larger community of learning that includes the past, the natural world, and the wisdom tradition that can be passed through you into the future. These stories of others' experiences spiral through our own lives, pre-

Trust in what you love, continue to do it, and it will take you where you need to go. And don't worry too much about security. You will eventually have a deep security when you begin to do what you want.

—Natalie Goldberg, *Writing Down the Bones*

senting the lessons from a new angle. Then we can grasp them intuitively, opening our minds to comprehend multiple meanings and connections we may not have noticed in other ways.

As you settle a little deeper into wherever you are right now, let's "talkstory" about how to use this information. The stories that follow are condensed versions of actual collaborative learning sessions between Andy and me and people of each thinking pattern who attended a workshop in the past decade. They are offered to illustrate the implications and applications of learning to use one's mind in its natural way. All names and identifying personal characteristics have been changed.

Independence is the developed capacity to adequately care for ourselves instead of clinging to others for protection.

—Sheldon Kopp,
*Raise Your Right Hand
Against Fear*

AVK: Tame It and Aim It

A woman discovers how she can use her visually triggered alpha mind to keep her from overwhelming others with a verbal onslaught and herself with an attack of overactive imagination.

Betsy was a career counselor in one of our supervision groups, a wiry woman in her middle fifties with a sharp and biting humor. She presented her problem in a rapid fire of precise language.

"One of the things I've been noticing at work recently is that after I've been conversing with people for a short period, their pupils dilate, and they disconnect their attention. I get extremely judgmental with myself for boring them. Then my awkwardness emerges and I feel completely off balance."

"I want to make sure I understand you, Betsy," I responded. "Let's create that same situation here. Listen carefully to your thinking process while I get one of those blank looks. Just notice what you tell yourself and what kinds of pictures flash in your mind."

She began her conversation in a straightforward manner. I immediately spaced out.

"Hmm, well, that's interesting. It's a little strange to slow my process down so much, but I'm telling myself that I'm even boring you, and then I'm flashing pictures as if I'm looking at me through your eyes, as if I were a hidden camera behind your head. Inside my head, in a snippy kind of a voice that reminds me of my mother's,

I'm saying that I'm making a fool of myself, and that I have a motor mouth. That crumples me inside. Very familiar, if I do say so myself."

"OK. So you are doing what you've always done and getting what you've always gotten. This time let's do it another way. When you see the glazed look in my eyes, keep looking out through your **own** eyes as you breathe. Tell me exactly what you're seeing. Instead of ascribing meaning to what you see, ask me what's going on. Do you understand what I'm saying?"

"Sure. OK. I'm talking on and on and now your eyes are glazing over. I'm seeing your mouth go kind of slack, your eyelids flutter, your fingers wiggle in your lap, and your foot begin to shake. I see your eyes shift away, and I look at your hands, and I begin to imagine you are not paying attention to me and are bored. Is that true, Dawna, are you bored?"

"Since you had the courage to ask, Betsy, I'll answer you straight and honestly. I'm not bored at all. When I hear a lot of words from anyone, I need to move and look away in order to absorb what I'm hearing. If I stare directly at you, I space out and stop paying attention."

"OK, that's fine. But what if someone tells me he or she **is** bored? That would be crushing."

"When you crush grapes you get wine. When you crush seeds you get oil. If people tell you they are bored, you can ask them what **would** be interesting to them at that particular moment. It might just be that their unconscious minds are triggered by the auditory channel and can't take in any more information without some silence. If you keep looking out of your own eyes instead of shifting into imaginative torture films in the drive-in movie theatre of your mind, you'll begin to see the very first cues of that.

"The habitual way you used is a great process for creating. If you want to write a poem about a tree, for instance, you can look at an elm, and let your mind begin to imagine what it must feel in a thunderstorm, and write from the elm's perspective. It works quite well for creating. It just is awful for relating!"

Children's needs are best met by grown-ups whose needs are met.

—Jean Clarke

AKV: From Vesuvius to Stradivarius

A gifted lawyer discovers how his kinesthetically triggered alpha mind intuitively opens and closes the possibility for greater intimacy.

Sarge is a large, well-built attorney with fiercely blue darting eyes, and a flattish aspect to his face. His body movements seem to punctuate his fluent, intense words.

"What I love the best about what I do is negotiating on the phone where I don't have to be seen. When I am in the courtroom I sometimes feel like a pressure cooker. The other attorneys can bat words back and forth with little or no effect, but I feel every word. I'm too sensitive," he said with great intensity.

"It happened at lunch today. I went to a Syrian place with Betsy, who's also an attorney, and we got into an argument about restaurants. The next thing I knew, I had bolted and was running downtown. It was as if my body just exploded and took over. I finally found myself in a music store, caressing a violin."

I moved next to Sarge so he wouldn't have to look directly at me. After briefly explaining how the AKV thinking pattern his mind used worked, I said, "Let's assume your body is the spokesperson for your intuition. It was trying to bring a very important question to your awareness when it took you to that music store. What would that be?"

He stared off into space for a long moment, one hand mindlessly stroking his Dick Tracy jaw. "An interesting thought just ran through my mind. I don't understand what this has to do with running to the store, but it is one I'm very interested in: 'What do I need to know about myself so I can open up and have more intimacy in my life?'"

"Fine. Now let's assume that your body was also answering that question. What would be going on in your life if you treated yourself the way you treated that violin?"

He shrugged. "I'm not sure I understand what you mean. I stroked it and played it a little, listened to the timbre and quality it produced. It was a fine, well-made instrument."

"Right, and if you considered **yourself** a fine and well-made

---

Finally you understand that the real motorcycle you are working on is yourself.

—Robert M. Pirsig,
Zen and the Art of Motorcycle Maintenance

instrument instead of a 'too-sensitive' man ...? If you listened to the sensations in your body and followed them, as if they were the vibrations of your soul? If you were to move whenever your body wanted you to move? If you were to allow your eyes to close or to roam as you would if you were playing a fine violin instead of forcing them to make contact?"

"It's an interesting idea. I'd have to try it out to know for sure if it would work."

I asked Betsy to come over and stand across from Sarge and begin to argue with him again. She had no difficulty at all with this task. Whatever Sarge said, she contradicted, and as her voice began to rise and push, he began to walk slowly around, looking away, rubbing his jaw, stretching and twisting his body. His words reverberated with intensity. Betsy began to mumble and then got quiet. She nodded and the argument was over.

Sarge threw his head back and bellowed. "That felt wonderful. My rage began again when Betsy was arguing, but as soon as I moved and looked away, it eased and felt more like passion. I was no longer afraid to engage with her or to get close. Amazing!"

"You are indeed. The way your instrument works, when you listen, the conscious mode of your mind is triggered and begins to open. When you sit still, your middle mind continues opening, and when you try to make eye contact by looking steadily at someone, your unconscious mind opens fully. The intensity of the other person's words slips in very deeply. This may be wonderful when making love, but in ordinary communication, it leaves you too absorptive.

"Movement becomes a filter. Being able to choose how deeply to receive someone may make you feel a lot safer with intimacy. I rest my case, Mr. Stradivarius."

> Commitment means, "I am going to stick with you and support your experience of well-being." Attachment means, "I am stuck without you."
> —Stewart Emery

VAK: Paralysis by Analysis

Using a new conscious perspective, a teacher learns a new way to float in the unconscious kinesthetic sea of her feelings instead of drowning in them.

One has not only an ability to perceive the world, but an ability to alter one's perception of it; more simply, one can change things by the manner in which one looks at them.

—Tom Robbins,
*Even Cowgirls
Get the Blues*

Anna's tortoise shell glasses seemed to form a windshield for her enormous brown eyes. As she spoke, her thin face, framed by flaming red hair, mirrored her rapid and energetic words.

"My problem is that I keep over-analyzing everything, Dawna. Since I've been in this workshop, I've been hearing people talk about all their feelings, but I'm not even sure I have any. Well, maybe I get pissed off once in a while, but that's it." Her chest caved inward, as if someone had poked a sharp finger there once too often.

"I tire myself out by analyzing, categorizing, until I'm caught in the same old vicious cycle, a hamster in a cage. I can't sleep at night even though I'm exhausted. But I don't know any other way to be with myself."

She softened as she spoke, as if finding the right words had somehow begun to relieve an invisible pressure.

"It's clear you don't belong in any kind of a cage, Anna," I said. "When a person is frustrated the way you are, it usually indicates that his or her subconscious mind is stuck. What I hear you saying is that you've been talking and talking to yourself in the same old way and getting the same old results. Is that right?"

She shook her head. "Exactly. Then I start to get frantic and scramble around doing anything to shut my mind up. Sometimes what's easiest is just to get lost in the television."

"It seems that frantic scrambling keeps you from noticing all of those confusing feelings. Talking fast would serve the same purpose. And the television shuts out any feelings that might get carried forward in words. If you could see another way, I'm sure you'd use it." I paused. She was right with me, nodding. "As a child, what did you learn about how to be yourself while you were feeling different kinds of emotions?"

"Are you kidding? My mother was angry all the time and the only thing my father felt was drunk."

"Well, how could you have learned to respond to any other feeling then?"

"I guess I couldn't. Maybe that's what I'm trying to do by watching all that television. But I'm not a child anymore," she said.

"Let's shift to another mode of thinking about this so you can get a different perspective. Draw me a quick sketch that represents you in that vicious cycle, categorizing and over-analyzing instead of feeling."

Anna grabbed black and red crayons and without thinking, put both of them in one hand and scrawled a tight spiral. When she was finished, she pushed the newsprint a few feet in front of her, throwing the crayons aside.

I responded immediately. "That's right. In fact, push it even farther away, Anna, so far that you can look at it with curiosity and even a little compassion, the way you were looking at other people in this circle all afternoon. In fact, get up and walk around so you can see it without feeling all of it."

Arms crossed over her chest, Anna backed up and paced a wide circle around the newsprint, glancing at it, tilting her head to one side and then to the other.

"It looks like a snail curling in on itself, its smooth body all bruised from scraping on the concrete. It has no shell and it's scared."

"From this perspective, and what you've learned from teaching kids, how would you respond to that creature?"

She walked slowly to the drawing, and then just sat down directly on top of it, her arms still wrapped around herself. She began to rock slowly, round and round. With the motion came silent tears.

"So now you've found another way to go in circles when you're feeling something—a way that seems a lot more compassionate and comforting than a hamster cage."

"It makes me think of when I was little and scared because my parents were yelling at me. They'd send me into my room. I'd crawl into bed, pull my blanket over my head so no one could see me, and tell myself stories. I used to wish that blanket was a hard shell so it could protect me from the hands that used to hit me." She paused and stared into space. "What did I used to call that blanket? I had it until I was eight or nine." Something clicked in her mind, her eyes refocused and she sat straight up. "I know. I called it, 'Liza!' I don't remember why I called it that, but Liza was the name of that blanket. I haven't thought of it in years!"

I wasn't going to say anything, but I couldn't resist. Smiling, I

The Indians long ago knew that music was going on permanently and that hearing it was like looking out a window at a landscape which didn't stop when one turned away.

—John Cage

responded, "When I see you like that Anna, holding yourself and rocking around in circles, I keep hearing the word 'over-analyzing.' What do you hear when I say that?"

Her face lit up, sunrise on an April morning.

"That's weird . . . I never realized . . . it sounds to me as if you're saying 'over Anna, Liza-ing,' which is what I feel like when I'm safe, as if my old blanket Liza is over me, covering me with comfort. What a strange coincidence!"

"Maybe. But maybe your unconscious mind has been trying to communicate something to you about how you can be with yourself when you're feeling all those emotions that don't have words. Maybe it's been trying to suggest to your subconscious mind that you need comfort!"

Anna shook her head, bemused. "This is quite amazing!"

I couldn't hold myself back. "Yes, Anna, you certainly are!"

VKA: From Carousel to Compass

A film editor learns a new strategy to use her mind to live her life from the inside out at her own rhythm instead of as a hyperactive, critical movie director.

"To me, my life often looks like a merry-go-round that keeps spinning faster and faster until everything's a blur. When I went on a walk after lunch and followed my mind the way you suggested Dawna, I took off my shoes and felt so peaceful, centered, I guess you'd call it. Obviously, my mind was working in a different way, but I don't know how to make it do that in my daily life. So ... now what?"

Jennifer's eyes left me no escape. They were bright, present, insistent—all I could notice until she moved. Though she must have been in her late forties, her walk was wide and open, almost childlike in its ease.

Her silver-haired husband Jim fidgeted next to her, legs crossed at the knees. I decided to begin with a metaphor she was familiar with.

"Each time your mind shifts in function, it's like a computer

A dog is not considered a good dog because he is a good barker. A man is not considered a good man because he is a good talker.

—Chuang Tzu

switching to another software program. The language it uses to organize experience is visual, but the language that triggers it into sorting
is kinesthetic, right?"

Again, she nodded without hesitation. "The way you describe
your process, it seems you lose your center by habitually stepping
outside and watching yourself and running a commentary on how
'Jennifer' is doing."

Continuing to nod as I spoke gave me the signal to keep going.
"From what you said, when you went for that walk you stayed inside
your own skin, seeing out through your own eyes. By taking off your
shoes, you caused yourself to notice the feel of the grass under your
feet, keeping you aware and kinesthetically receptive. What happened to the voices in your head when you were simply walking
down the road?"

My question seemed to startle her. She shook her head a bit, ran
a long finger across her lips. Her hands began to move before her
mouth did, as if they were painting the words before they were spoken. "Well, I guess it got very quiet. I heard the birds, my feet
crunching, just what was going on around me. The only other time
I really feel that peaceful and relaxed is when I'm dancing to music I
love. I close my eyes and float to it."

"So shutting out the world visually increases your receptivity in
the widest mode of your mind, auditorily. It's as if the music moves
your body and then images flow through your mind. The mental
merry-go-round works in a similar manner but with a very different
effect. You hear people tell you what to do: 'Jennifer, it's time to do
this,' 'Jennifer, I need this,' 'Jennifer, when are you going to do this?'
and each voice pulls you in a different direction. I imagine that's as
uncomfortable as being a rope in a tug-of-war, so you stop feeling
your body as quickly as possible. You watch everything spin around
as if it were a little metal merry-go-round pulled to turning in one
direction by a magnet on the left and then in another direction by a
magnet on the right, and then ..."

"Stop please, Dawna, I'm getting nauseated. That's exactly what
it's like. For years I've tried to show Jim that's just how I get overloaded. It gets so bad I just collapse and stare blindly into space. I

> What it amounts to is that
> I'm scared of being alone
> with what I feel.
> —Doris Lessing,
> *The Golden Notebook*

My loneliness was like a letter I carried with me, and glanced at nervously, and folded and unfolded, but never read; a letter I gave instead to every woman who ever loved me as if this clue to my longing were addressed to her, as if I didn't recognize in the rise and fall of the writing, my own hand.

—Sy Syfransky,
The Sun. December, 1989

used to take Valium, but that made me feel so numb I got totally lost." She immediately leaned over and patted Jim on the shoulder as if to reassure him. "Do you have any ideas what I can do about it?"

I wasn't sure whether she was addressing her question to me or Jim, but I jumped in. "So what Valium did was to numb out your kinesthetic sorting mind, leaving you calmer but unable to navigate at all according to your **own** compass, is that right? It just made you more pliant?"

She nodded emphatically.

"OK, let's try a simple experiment. Sit still right there for a few minutes, and Andy and I will each tell you what we want you to do. You keep looking at us as usual."

Jennifer nodded and Andy and I strolled around, asking her to do this, to look at that, to fix this, to notice that. She watched as if she were at the finals of Wimbledon. After several minutes, she held up both her hands, and squeezed her eyes shut. Nearly shouting, she insisted we stop.

"I hate that. I stop seeing anything, everything blurs, my neck gets tense and my hands get instantly cold and clammy."

"What do you imagine your neck and hands are trying to tell you? If your hands had words what would they be saying?"

"Well, when I get hot, it usually means 'yes, do it, go for it,' so I guess cold means 'no' in some way. I haven't ever thought about it before, but they **do** get cold and clammy whenever I feel over-whelmed. So do my feet. It's as if my energy leaves them."

"OK, let's do it another way. We'll continue overwhelming as before, but this time you get up and simply walk around, noticing your breath and the visual details of the room around you, the way you did outside. **We** won't change at all. All that will change will be the way you respond **to** us."

Andy and I repeated our obnoxious litany, but Jennifer walked slowly around the room, looking at us and then away, her breath even and steady, her eyes vibrant.

"That's the strangest, most wonderful thing, Dawna. It's as if I have my own place. Your voices are there and I hear them, but they don't feel like darts coming at me. I see each of you so clearly I could sketch you. It's quite simple, but absolutely amazing!" She put her hands on her hips and stared down at her bare feet. "I bet they were trying to tell me to move all along, and my hands were saying to touch myself, to **feel** my own warmth instead of **doing** things so frenetically! Is that what you think?"

"What I think doesn't really matter, does it? That seems to be what your body thinks. When you just sit or stand still, you absorb all those words and directions into your captive unconscious mind, and your navigational compass begins to spin wildly."

"Aha! Now I know why, when Jim tells me all the things I need to do first thing in the morning, before I have a chance to make up my own list, I go nuts. Seeing that list organizes me and gives me my own magnetic north. I'm sure that Jim's mind is AKV, because he needs to talk things out to feel organized, and hates to write anything down. I do it for him. Obviously, all I need to do is ask him to wait until I've finished my own map. Can sanity really be such a simple thing?"

Before I could say a word, she put her hand over my mouth. "Don't answer that one, please Dawna, I'd like to live with it myself for a while."

All I could do was smile. "May that question be a finger pointing in a new direction, Jennifer."

> Good for the body is the work of the soul, and good for the soul is the work of the body, and good for either is the work of the other.
>
> —Henry David Thoreau

KVA: Untying the Knots

Milton Erickson said that a powerful mind can take a resource from one experience and smoothly transfer it for use in another aspect of that person's life. A man learns how to do this using his kinesthetic skills to help his verbally sensitive theta mind.

Alan came to work with me because he "tied himself in knots" every time he had to speak in front of a group of people. (Anything more than one person represented a group.) He was a slim, tanned man, who reminded me of pine forests and L.L. Bean catalogs. He told me that what he remembered most about school was having to stand up and read out loud.

"If I heard it once, I heard it a thousand times: 'Alan, you have to get over being so shy.' At first, I didn't even know what shy meant, but people always seemed to attach that word to my name, 'Shy-alan.' I'd try to force myself to speak, and I could manage it with one, or on rare occasions, two other people, but if I was made to stand up in front of a group of two or more, I'd just be tied up in one huge knot. And that's still exactly what happens to me."

Since Alan's mind used the KVA pattern, I knew he must be short-circuiting someplace between the subconscious and unconscious modes of his mind. I asked him about the resources in his life, the things he loved to do and did well. He told me how he often went canoeing by himself on the Allagash River. This provoked a question in my mind.

"Alan, I've never gone on a long canoe trip, but I've always wondered what you do when there's a strong current and you want to pull over to shore for lunch or some such thing. How do you keep your canoe from being washed away?"

He shrugged. "That's easy Dawna. I just pull the bow up on shore and tie it with a line to a nearby tree."

"Having never done such a thing myself, I have a dumb question: what kind of knot do you use?"

"Well, I use an ordinary slip knot, of course."

"Why a slip knot?"

He rolled his eyes upward. "It's the simplest kind. When I want to leave, I just pull on the rope and it's untied, ready to go. But what's this got to do with my being so shy, Dawna?"

Rather than answer his question, I handed him some clothesline from my desk drawer. "Make the kind of knot you would tie yourself into if you were going to speak to a group of 40 glaring experts."

"Come on Dawna, I was only using that as a figure of speech."

Even as he protested, his long, slim fingers were deftly twisting and looping the rope.

"What do you call that kind of knot?" I asked.

"It's, ummm, a square knot, I guess." he replied.

I grabbed one end and pulled. The whole knot tightened immediately. "No wonder you have trouble speaking! Here's what I suggest you do. Take this little rope with you. The next time you have to make a presentation to a group of people, tie a slip knot in it. Just before you speak, hold the rope, look at the knot, ask yourself what you really want to say, and pull one end, the way you do with your canoe."

Three years later, Alan is making presentations with ease to groups large and small. He tells me that he still carries the rope in his pocket, and goes through the tying and untying ritual before each talk!

When I was a kid I drew like Michaelangelo. It took me years to learn to draw like a kid.

—Pablo Picasso

KAV: Giving Without Giving Herself Away

A woman learns how to make empathetic contact by receiving another person through each mode of her mind rather than abandoning herself to enter them sympathetically.

The hottest question asked in a recent West Coast Study Group was, "How do I pay attention to my own needs when I'm with another person?" Julia had been leaning in all morning, opening her mouth as if to speak, and then clamping it shut. Finally, a half-hour before lunch, her arm began to wave as if it were a willow branch in a stiff wind.

"Dawna, I'm just stunned. I've been realizing that I only know how to be with people if I crawl inside them, put my mind inside their body to figure out what **they** need. Until this morning, I thought that was normal, how you were supposed to care about a person. I **always** feel the other person, but I think I never feel myself."

Observing that Julia's mind used the KAV pattern, I realized that starting with an experience would be the most effective way to approach her question.

"Let's make that happen now, OK Julia? Make contact with me in your habitual way."

She approached as if she were liquid wax melting into me. I began to rock back and forth unconsciously. She followed my rhythm exactly, casually placing a hand on my shoulder. Before proceeding, I thought we'd better check in.

"Ok, Julia, how are you feeling now?"

"To be honest, Dawna, I haven't the foggiest idea ... I've already done it. I left myself somehow, and began feeling what **you** were feeling, kind of happy and curious and intent. That's what I do all the time. But when I get alone, I'm empty and don't feel anything."

"I think I understand. Since your mind uses the KAV pattern, what you are doing is receiving me through your kinesthetic channel by touching me and moving to my rhythm. Then you ask me a question while staring at me, and immediately answer it by pouring into me as if your arm were a hose on a gas pump."

Her hand slid back to her side, her eyes to her own feet. "That's probably right, but I'm sick of being everyone else's filling station and having my own tanks run on empty. I haven't the foggiest idea what **I** need."

"Of course. Julia, let's try an experiment. Let's use the mechanism of the problem as the mechanism of finding yourself. This time when you touch me, Julia, imagine your arm is a drinking straw. Tell yourself you'll bring me **into** you instead of the other way around. OK?"

She nodded wordlessly, and again rested her hand on my shoulder. This time, though, it seemed to be floating on a layer of air, as she asked me, "How are you feeling, Dawna?"

"Well, since you asked, not so good. I've been sitting for a long time, and I'm kind of stiff. My back feels like cardboard. How about you, Julia?"

"Interesting. I'm feeling solid and tingly, awake actually, for the first time all morning. Very interesting, but it can't be this simple can it? What if I'm not touching you, what then?"

I began to rock back and forth, and as Julia instinctively followed me, I pushed gently against her chest. She wobbled backwards, off balance.

"There, Julia, were you beginning to lose yourself again?"

She nodded, smiling as if she'd been caught licking cake frosting off a finger.

"Make sure that you are moving in your **own** rhythm so you don't attach your hose nozzle to my pump. If you stay with yourself, you'll know what you want, need, think, and feel. If you lose contact with that conscious channel, you've stopped accessing the aspect of your mind that helps you discriminate what's you and what's not you." I looked curiously at her for a signal to go on. She was nodding to my words.

"The same thing happens when a person gets stoned on marijuana and becomes one with everyone and everything else. Your habitual way of joining another is useful in your work as a movement therapist and artist. It probably helps you establish a wonderful rapport, but if you're going to leave your home territory so often, it seems important to have a map so you know how to come back to yourself."

Julia stretched her arms in the air and spun around as if she were skating on ice. Her eyes flashed while she spoke. "I certainly want to have a choice about all of this. My habit is to follow the most powerful energy around. I practice a martial art and as soon as I touch my partner I lose my center. I can follow but never lead. It's one of the main reasons I haven't respected myself. Up until now, the only way I knew how not to do it was to withdraw or numb out with cocaine. Using my **arm** as a straw seems a much healthier alternative!"

"Receiving another person **that** way is called empathy rather than sympathy. You'll find yourself curious about when you had a similar experience to what the other person is going through, when you felt like that, said something like that, how it worked for you, how it worked against you. Rather than isolating yourself by trying to keep a 'clinical distance,' you'll be connecting on a deep and compassionate level without having to abandon or betray yourself."

"Let me guess what you're going to say next, Dawna. I can tell you and stay in my own body. I bet the words that were going to come out of your mouth were, 'It's really quite simple, but not necessarily easy!' Am I right?"

There was nothing else I could say. Laughter brought the learning home to all of us.

The next message you need is always right where you are.

—Ram Dass

Respecting Ourselves

Each of these stories is illustrative of bringing home to oneself the kind of curiosity that opens us to possibility rather than tranquilizing us into an old familiar limited identity. We begin to respect our need to look away, for silence, or movement. We begin to be curious about how we can give ourselves more space to explore in an alpha state of mind, more freedom in theta, more structure in beta. We begin to use the confidence we feel in one symbolic language to support the hesitancy we experience in another. Developing this kind of relationship with our own minds ensures that we will bring a new openness to our relationships with others and the world.

In order to understand what another person is saying, you must assume it is true, and try to imagine what it is true of.

—George Miller, cognitive scientist

CHAPTER 12

PARTNERING THE POSSIBLE: CONNECTING WITH OTHERS

*'I see the dog'—with this sentence structure,
'I' is the center of the universe. We forget in
our language structure that while 'I' look at the
dog,' 'the dog' is simultaneously looking at us.
It is interesting to note that in the Japanese
language the sentence would say, 'I dog seeing.'
There is an exchange or interaction rather than
a subject acting on an object.*

—Natalie Goldberg,
Writing Down the Bones

This chapter is designed to help you apply the knowledge you have gained about personal thinking patterns to your relationships with others. It offers specific suggestions and practices for communicating with compassion, as well as skills to translate your message into another person's native tongue.

The Art of Communication

Once people begin to understand how to utilize the information about the particular pattern their own mind uses to process information, they usually come to a "corner" in their thinking. I can tell they are there because they lean forward, furrow their brow, and begin the next sentence with the word "but." "But Dawna, how in the world can we communicate anything to anyone else, knowing that we all use different patterns to think? What are teachers supposed to do, or managers? How do we deal with a partner whose mind uses a totally different pattern than ours? Does this mean that we should find friends and lovers who have the same pattern as ours?"

At one level, communication seems much easier if we assume we all play our mental instruments in the same way. You just treat someone else the way you want to be treated and there should be no problem, right? Of course not. Let's go back to the metaphor of the orchestra. It probably would be easier on the conductor, the musicians and the audience if everyone played a harmonica, right? Of course not. Understanding our mental diversity may make the complexity of human interaction more difficult, but who would want to give up the richness of that diversity?

It does require, however, that we release ourselves from some very basic assumptions we have about how other people function, and open ourselves to a perpetual inquiry into how the other person is perceiving the world and how we can blend in harmony with him or her.

It also demands that we continually tune and re-tune our own instrument, by asking, "How can I be available to myself and my needs, while simultaneously being available to reach out in curiosity to others?"

This question seems to be at the source of every communication gap that I've encountered in both organizational and personal relationships.

The bridge you can build to cross this gap has two approach ramps: two basic practices that bring you to the place where minds

Love alone is capable of uniting living beings in such a way as to complete and fulfill them, for it alone takes them and joins them by what is deepest in themselves.

—Teilhard de Chardin

can meet in resonance. The first is drawn from the martial art of aiki-do, and entails finding yourself with another. The second, entering another's model of the world, involves being willing to turn and find the other with you.

You begin by finding yourself. This means coming fully present, all of your molecules constellating around your center of balance—feeling your body, bringing the world in through your eyes and ears. This means finding what in aikido they call your "virtuous intent." What do you need, what's important to you in the moment?

When I ask these last questions to people stuck in a conflict situation, they often respond, "Well I want him to..." or "My intent is for her to.." These responses imply that for you to move in the direction you desire, the other person must change. This ultimately will mean you must manipulate him or her into doing what you want. Since this is a fruitless and frustrating approach, consider the alternative—taking the time and effort to discover what's really important to you in that moment, where you want to go, what you need to do so that you will be true to your heart.

The following practice is an extension of what you learned in the last chapter, framed to help you find yourself and your intent. It involves balancing your mind in the presence of another. It should take only minutes, and is equally effective if you are calm or sitting right on the edge of a "sizzle point," the moment of choice right before a fight takes off with an energy of its own and seems irreversible and your adrenaline starts to pump. It's a moment of power when you make the choice to center yourself or to lose it.

> It's not enough to study them like beetles under a microscope; you need to know what it feels like to be a beetle.
>
> —Roger Fisher & William Ury, *Getting To Yes*

Practice:
Centering—Finding Yourself with Another

- *All you have to do is choose to increase your awareness of the information your senses are giving you in that moment, and name it out loud: "Right now, my mouth is dry, I can feel my hands clenched, I can hear my teeth grinding, I can see your eyes squinting at me, and your glasses steaming." That's it!*

*Remember to notice and name **just** the information each sense perceives.*

Refuse to allow, for those minutes, interpretations such as, "I hear you growling, and that's because you can't control that awful temper you inherited from your father..." Refuse to allow the inner horror stories, the drive-in movies, the habitual feelings. This is not a time for creative thinking such as, "You are chewing on that pencil because you'd really like to tear my head off the way you always do when..."

Rather than try to control your energy or be controlled by it, just name it. That naming will open your throat and soften your heart, allowing your energy to find a place in the world.

- *The next step is to ask yourself "What do I need right now? What is my intention?" Do not proceed with further contact until you know. A heat-seeking missile without a target will go for the warmest thing around.*

It takes a golden ear to be empty enough of itself to hear clearly.

—M.C. Richards (KVA), *Centering*

Entering Another's Model Of the World

Once you are clear about where you are and where you want to go, once you hear your own inner voice and can feel your own direction, *then* you can expand in curiosity toward the other person. You can become very curious about his or her intent. What's this other person's model of the world like? How is he or she perceiving? What would it feel like to be that person, to see the world through his or her eyes? How would he or she understand the current moment?

This may seem more complex than it is. Think about two jazz musicians or two actors improvising, two people playing a pick-up game of basketball, a couple doing the samba on a dance floor or playing charades at a party. In order to be effective, they must enter each other's model of the world while maintaining their own center. You become a wood carver working with a piece of mahogany. How can you go with the grain and still carve the design you hold in your mind? How can you support the other and receive support from the other? How can you interconnect?

Relationship always seems to involve this balancing and blending of learning what you need to do or say to be true to your heart **and** being willing to enter someone else's model of the world to discover what it's like for them.

This may be simple, but it is not easy. As an example of what is involved, I'd like to share a story with you of a couple I worked with. I'll call them Marie and Rick. They had been together for fifteen years, fourteen of which were miserable. They had been in and out of psychotherapy for a decade. Rick's mind used the AKV pattern, Marie's the VKA. What they had learned in therapy was that she needed him to listen and he wouldn't listen to her. She had been complaining that for fourteen years whenever she said something, he'd roll his eyes back, and say it was dumb. He kept complaining that she gave him the silent treatment or talked around in circles about things that didn't mean anything.

Understanding the differences in how their minds processed experience should have helped. It didn't. They were interested, but each used the information to prove the case they had been building so meticulously all those years. "So there you go again not listening to me just like the typical insensitive AKV!" Marie whined. "What are you talking about, I'm listening, but you never hear what I'm saying, you just say I'm triggering your theta mind and space out like a dumb-dumb."

It is very important to me that this system be used as a tool not a weapon, but to tell you the truth, I had no idea how to be effective with Marie and Rick. I was about to give up. They came to my office for what was supposed to be the last session. When they entered, I was playing a piece of classical music neither of them had ever heard. It was one of my favorites—a string quartet by Haydn—a model for a magnificent conversation between different instruments. It was so lovely I couldn't bear to turn it off and I invited them to sit and listen with me for the first five minutes of our session.

When it was finished, Marie commented, "All those lovely waterfalls and birds! The green grass, the meadows!" Rick immediately replied, "What are you talking about? Couldn't you hear how the violin and the cello came together during that interval and ... (he went on for five minutes with a detailed analysis of the piece)." I

> The test of a first-rate intelligence is the ability to hold two opposed ideas in the mind at the same time, and retain the ability to function.
>
> —F. Scott Fitzgerald

commented on how astounding it was that each of them had listened to the same piece of music but heard it in such different ways. I wondered what would happen if they would listen through each others' ears. The comment was bizarre enough to stun them into confusion long enough to make a suggestion.

"Why don't you sit back to back with each other. I'm going to play the same music again. You know how you heard it and what effect it had on you. This time listen as if you were your partner. Listen the way he or she did. Listen through his or her model of the world. Listen with curiosity about what it would be like to hear that way. Forget trying to prove anything. Just be curious about what it's like for the other."

I listened as if the right ear could hear his way and the left ear could hear her way. At the end of five minutes, Rick's face was soft and his chest was wide, Marie's face was alert, her posture straight, vital. He spoke first. "Is that how you hear the world? Do you hear me like that when I speak? I never knew. I heard things I never hear when I listen to music—the connections, the interplay! It was quite magical really. Is that how you hear me?"

Marie nodded wordlessly, stroking his cheek and then said, "I always longed to be able to understand what was happening to create that incredible sound that made me feel the way I feel when I listen to music. I never have before. But this time, this time, I didn't get lost in the music. I could hear it, and simultaneously I could understand it. What an amazing experience!"

Haydn and the experience of being able to enter another's model of the world built a bridge of compassion between them that no therapist could ever create.

Meeting of the Minds

Many of the differences between us that we believe to be clashing personality traits are actually a result of the different operational characteristics of our particular thinking patterns. The tools of working with these differences all require that you replace trying to manipulate the other with learning to flexibly maneuver yourself so

We must be continuously on our watch for ways in which we may enlarge our consciousness.

—Aldous Huxley

that you can meet their mind where it is.

"Why should I be the one to bend?" I asked the sensei in my first year of studying aikido. He gently pushed against my shoulder. I resisted. He responded, "Because you have the gift of knowing many options of response." He paused just long enough for me to wonder what those were, then he pushed again. This time I turned aside as if I were a revolving glass door. He smiled. "Just so," he said, "Now the choice is yours, yes?"

This doesn't mean giving up yourself or your own point of view. For example, if I want to make contact with my father-in-law (KVA), I don't have to feel what he feels or even agree with his beliefs in an attempt to make him like me. Instead, I can feel my desire to connect with him in my center, respect the experiences he already has, and link with those as a way of fostering understanding between us. He loves to sail, and was a naval flight instructor in World War II. Since that's where his passion and resources are, those are the metaphors and images I'll draw from when I want to communicate something to him. If I'm trying to explain, for instance, how difficult writing can be at times, I might talk about how it feels to stall out in a plane or become becalmed in a sailboat.

This joining is **not** done as a communication trick. It is respectful and natural. It simply requires becoming curious about what the other person already knows, how he or she perceives the world, and how to connect to the perceptual pattern of the other person.

> You must understand the whole of life, not just one little part of it. That is why you must read, that is why you must look at the skies, that is why you must sing, and dance, and write poems, and suffer, and understand, for all that is life.
>
> —J. Krishnamurti
> *Think On These Things*

Practice: Building a Bridge of Compassion

You can use your understanding of thinking patterns to build that bridge by translating their experience into yours. For example, let's say your mind uses the AVK pattern and the other person's uses the KVA. And let's say their silences drive you crazy. How can they be so quiet?

You can build the bridge of compassion by exploring your own experience of what it is like to be so still, to take touch in so deeply. If you don't understand why it is so hard for that person to be quiet once in a while, imagine what it would be like for you to have to function with your eyes shut. Or if your KAV work partner presents you with a written report that is a day late and you are ready to throw it across the room, perhaps you could cross the bridge by imagining you had made a model with your hands and gave it to someone who was about to throw it into a corner in frustration because of how long overdue it was.

This translation back and forth is what is meant by entering another person's model of the world and what follows is the most basic and important material you can use to build that bridge to others' minds.

The Language of Power, the Power of Language

When was the last time you were trying to communicate with someone, and that's what it was—**trying.** You knew you weren't getting your point across, or the other person wasn't getting his or her point across. Perhaps it was because of a stunning headache or because you were on your way to have a root canal. It may have been that Mercury was in retrograde in your astrological chart. It's also just possible that what produced that communication gap was that your point and the other person's point were spoken in two different perceptual languages. That's because the words we use will trigger different responses from different modes in someone's mind.

Entering another's model of the world is a lot like entering another person's home. Think of their conscious mind as entering through the front door to the living room, their subconscious state of mind as being in the kitchen, and their unconscious state of mind as being in their bedroom. Almost everyone knows that the most polite way is to enter the front door to the living room, then proceed to the kitchen and eventually, if you know them well, to the bedroom. Frequently when there's a communication gap, it's because getting to the point your way and getting to the point their way may have been in two completely different perceptual languages. The words we use can trigger each other into clarity, confusion, or wonder.

For anyone whose beta thinking is triggered by auditory information, for instance, words are the way to knock on the front door

You can only hope to find a lasting solution to a conflict if you have learned to see the other objectively, but at the same time, to experience their difficulties subjectively.

—Dag Hammarskjold, *Markings*

and enter their mind. "Getting to the point" means coming to words. Clear, precise, straightforward words. You'd use language like, "Let me tell you about..." or "Talk to you soon." You might choose vocabulary that emphasized the auditory quality of experience such as "orchestrate," "amplify," "discuss." You might tell them they ring your chimes. And you'd understand that the absence of contact would be described as being given "the silent treatment," and thus how important talking things over was to that person, and that to them chaos would be cacophony.

Likewise, if you were trying to get clear with someone whose beta thinking was triggered visually, you'd want to "look over" the subject with the person, to offer your perspective on it. You'd use language like "See you soon." or "Clearly, we see this from different angles." You might choose vocabulary that emphasized the visual quality of an experience such as "bright," "vague," "colorful." You might tell them that they light up your life. And you'd understand that the absence of contact would be described as "being left in the dark" and thus how important it is for them not to be left out of the picture. Chaos for them would be like a disco light show.

Knocking on the front door of someone whose beta thinking was triggered kinesthetically, you'd probably say "I just feel that..." and want to get in touch with, get a grasp on what is really happening. You might choose vocabulary that emphasized the kinesthetic quality of an experience, such as "struggle," "smooth," "comfort," "out of touch." You might tell them that they give you goose bumps. It would help to understand that they would describe their need for contact as an aversion to being given "the cold shoulder," and thus would need to straighten things out so they could keep in touch. Chaos would be a carnival ride or a roller coaster.

Whether you are presenting information to them in a business meeting or making love, the first place you want to communicate with a person, if possible, is in his or her conscious state of mind, because that's the place that will seem the most natural and comfortable. This is the most effective way to establish rapport with someone you've just met or someone you've known for years.

The magic of children is their ability to cloud our memories so that when we look back we recall only the golden moments, the sweet laughter and the sentimental tears, and none of the awful truths.

—Russell Baker

Overlapping: Developing Perceptual Fluency

The capacity to shift and translate into the language of another's model of the world—what I call "overlapping"—may seem awkward at first, but then it may also expand your horizons.

I have learned silence from the talkative, tolerance from the intolerant, and kindness from the unkind. yet starnge, I am ungrateful to these teachers.

—Kahlil Gibran

Practice: Awkward and Alive

Try something—cross your fingers and sit for a moment with your hands folded in the habitual way you always did as a child in school.

Now notice how they are folded. Is the right index finger over the left or the other way around? Unlace them and refold them in the reverse, nonhabitual way.

Go back and forth a few times and consider which way is more comfortable. Which way is more awkward? Which way are you more aware of the spaces between your fingers? Which way are your hands more alive?

Almost everyone concurs that the non-habitual, awkward way is also the way of increased awareness and the most aliveness. What our hands tell us is that even though it will be awkward at first to shift the way you are communicating from your customary or habitual language into someone else's, it can also increase the awareness and aliveness in your relationship. Practice makes it as automatic as it is to shift when you are communicating with your five year old, and then shift again when you speak to her forty-five-year-old mother. You barely have to think about it. You make the shift as a way of paying respect to each different model of the world, bridging the gap.

Practice: Overlapping

You can learn to make this crossing by communicating with yourself, either in writing or by talking to yourself out loud or on a tape recorder.

- *Briefly describe your most annoying current problem in your usual way. Notice the effect of doing that.*

- *Overlap to another perceptual language. Include images as well. If you began describing how the problem makes you feel and what you've been trying to do about it (kinesthetic), just slip into discussing the way it looks to you from your perspective (visual), or give the reasons you cannot talk about this (auditory).*

Pause and notice the effect that has on you.

- *Overlap to the third channel, and describe your problem through that symbolic language. Pause to notice the effect.*

  Obviously, as you change language, you'll also be changing consciousness. This practice gives your brain increased flexibility. You can practice overlapping the way you would stretch a muscle or sketch a favorite scene.

- *Now play with me. I'm listening to the wind in the trees. How would that translate into a kinesthetic experience? What way could you describe it visually so that we would be talking about the same thing?*

- *When you notice you're describing something, anything, a book you read or a day at the office, begin in your usual mode: "I saw Benjamin Rimplehouse today, dear, he looks awful. I told him we'd see about when we could ...."*

- *Then overlap to another channel: "He sounded just fine though. He asked if we'd like to go to a concert with him tonight, but I said we'd have to play it by ear ...."*

- *Then overlap again: "But the way he keeps scratching his head gives me the willies, so let's take one thing at a time..."*

> Man's mind is a mirror of a universe that mirrors man's mind.
>
> —Joseph Chilton Pearce

I'm wondering if you're starting to get a feel for this. Do you see the point? Am I telling you what you need to know?

Please note: The "further away" you get from **your** conscious mind, the wider you go in the spiral, the more awkward you may feel. But in the same way that folding your hands back and forth can get to be like a game, learning to overlap can also be quite enjoyable and can have a significant effect on how you listen to others who perceive and describe the world through a different natural intelligence.

You can increase this facility for perceptual fluency by doing casual research: find people whose brains use a different conscious channel language than yours. Be curious. Share an experience with them, and then listen as they describe what the same experience is like for them—walk in their shoes, see things through their eyes.

Or give them an object: a music box, a rock, a used tea bag, and ask them to describe it to you. Then give the same object to someone else whose conscious style is different, and ask for a description.

My favorite response came when I was learning to use language the way someone would whose beta thinking was triggered by words. I asked as many people of this persuasion as I could find to describe an orgasm. (Of course, I only asked people I knew well!) The winner was Anita: "A pulsating crescendo, culminating in a symphonic release of ecstasy and inhibition."

Suggestions for further casual research: go to a cafe, diner, or shopping mall and eavesdrop, observe, fool around. Watch a soap opera, listen to a talk show, play a pick-up game of softball, and notice which symbolic languages predominate. You can be quite subtle about all of this or very blatant. You can tell the person, for instance, that you are learning how to communicate with people whose minds work like theirs, and you need them to help you out.

What is most important is that you be curious. You may notice some very interesting things, beyond the language people use. For example, people who are visually smart tend to sit or stand across from someone so they can see them. Those who are body smart might smell their fingers or jiggle, or run their hands through their hair a lot, or put a hand on your shoulder.

Take a risk. Have them teach **you** something and describe the experience you're sharing in their beta language. "Gee George, this feels exciting. I know I keep dropping the ball on your foot, but I do think I'm getting the hang of this, don't you?"

If you get stuck, just ask them how they'd say it.

Take a bigger risk. Teach **them** something, something they'd like to learn that you know how to do. Teach it in little morsels, step by step. You don't even have to know anything about how their minds work when you begin. You will by the time you finish.

Start anyplace. Show someone or tell someone or have someone just do it. Ask that person how learning that step in that way affected him or her. Overlap to another channel. Notice the effect.

Each time we see the face…it is our own ideas of him which we recognize.

—Marcel Proust

Examples of Perceptual Language—Analogies

KINESTHETIC	VISUAL	AUDITORY
I just feel that...	The way it looks to me...	I tell myself...
Let's get in touch.	See you soon.	Talk to you later.
I can't get a handle on this at all.	Clearly, we have different perspectives.	You're talking out of both sides of your mouth.
struggle, smooth, comfort, grasp, tight, out of touch	bright, clear, vague, focus, flash, colorful, dark	harmonious, explain, orchestrate, tone, amplify, discuss
"You give me goose bumps."	"You light up my life."	"You ring my chimes."
still	dark	silent
roller coaster	disco light show	cacophany
crumbs in bed	messy room	fingernails on the chalkboard
get things straightened out	clear things up	talk things over
cold shoulder	left out of the picture	silent treatment

Overlap once more. Notice the effect. Ask again.

Be like a baby learning to grasp a cup for the first time. Disregard what doesn't work, do more of what does, until hand reaches cup—BINGO! Your friend will have learned what you're teaching, and both of you will have learned a great deal about how that friend's mind works.

Hug friend. Or speak words of appreciation. Or wink!

Developing perceptual fluency will increase your ability to access your total mind. No small thing. You will also find that habitual defensiveness and manipulation of others is gradually replaced by a flexible ability to establish rapport with a wide variety of people. What is needed to reach that point is lavish curiosity and the willingness to be a little awkward and embarrassed—qualities that indicate that we are, after all, merely human.

Respecting Perceptual Sensitivity

As we open our minds from the conscious state, the front door, to the unconscious, the bedroom, we progress from the most assertive state of mind to the most sensitive, from the most detailed to the most systemic and generative. You may remember that the wider or more expansive the state of mind, the more thinking becomes symbolic—words become songs and sounds and hums, letters become visions, actions become gut feelings or ideas of new ways to do something. Most importantly for communication, the person has less and less capacity to filter or screen out stimuli, and so the thinking becomes more and more receptive, intuitive, sacred.

Most of us fall into a communication abyss because we have so little awareness of this increased sensitivity. We live in an invasive culture where slapping someone on the back, putting words in their mouth, or showing them what a fool they're making of themselves is considered just good fun and anyone who doesn't enjoy it is considered oversensitive. Since the unconscious mind is the generator of innovation, the creator of new ideas, and the place from which we can perceive the whole of things, we very well may be polluting the very source of the wisdom we most need to survive as a species.

Because this is such an important aspect of communicating with others, I'd like to share with you how each of the six patterns describe in their own way how to treat them well with an awareness of their unique sensitivity. These descriptions were condensed from the words of thousands of people in different workshops and seminars when they gathered together to develop their own brief "Bill of Rights."

To Communicate Well with People Who Have "Bedroom Ears"—KVA, VKA

1. Give us lots of silence without pressure when you want us to respond to you.

2. Ask us questions that turn us back to ourselves, not to you: "What do you need?" is better than "How can I help?"

3. Ask us questions that help us see and find our options. Don't

> Using another as a means of satisfaction and security is not love. Love is never security; love is a state in which there is no desire to be secure; it is a state of vulnerability.
>
> —J. Krishnamurti

tell us what our choices are or ask us why we are doing what we're doing. Ask us where we want to go.

4. Don't ask us yes/no, either/or questions. We can find every variable between yes and no, either and or. We aren't binary computers.

5. Questions that work well are ones that use a gentle, curious tone of voice: tender, undemanding.

6. Tell us stories instead of telling us what to do. Teach us indirectly, like "I know a man who was having trouble fixing his flat tire..."

7. Do NOT answer our questions, no matter how seductively we try to get you to do so. Don't fill in our spaces with your words, either.

8. Offer us suggestions instead of giving us answers/orders.

> Something we were
> withholding made us
> weak until we found out
> it was ourselves.
>
> —Robert Frost

To Communicate Well with People Who Have "Bedroom Eyes"(KAV, AKV)

1. Don't keep telling us to look at things. Ask us if you can show us something.

2. Allow us to look wherever we want when we talk to you. Eye contact is deeply intimate.

3. Our feelings show in our bodies, not on our faces. Ask us what we're feeling.

4. Know that we write only rarely and only if we really care about what we're writing about.

5. Don't look at us with expectations or analytical eyes. Look as if you're looking at an animal in the woods.

6. Just because we look blank, don't make us into your movie screen. Check out if what you imagine about us is true.

To Communicate Well with People Who Have "Bedroom Bodies" (VAK, AVK)

1. Do things with us that are unstructured, so we can establish

and follow our own rhythm.

2. Touch us first in "public" places like a hand or a foot. Remember, touch isn't casual to us.

3. Don't touch us if you're trying to get something or if you aren't enjoying it. We'll know it.

4. It takes us longer to know what we feel but we feel very deeply.

5. Remember that we aren't really uncoordinated, we just need to be taught slowly, in small pieces with lots of metaphors and descriptions.

6. Understand that physical connections are extremely profound for us and we remember them for a very long time—the good ones and the bad ones.

7. Understand that we rarely like to do the same thing in the same way twice.

8. Understand that "fixing" things with our hands is a creative process that can cause us great frustration.

> To confront a person with his own shadow is to show him his own light.
>
> —Carl Jung

Relationship Permutations and Combinations of Thinking Patterns

People are always asking me which patterns are the most compatible with which. Sorry. Any musical instrument can make beautiful music with any other, if you understand how to tune and play them properly. In that spirit, it seems helpful to highlight some particular wisdom that has been gathered about the different permutations and combinations of thinking patterns.

When you and I communicate, the patterns our brains use can:

- be the same: "**A Match**," for example, AVK/AVK;

- have one channel in common: "**The Single Point**," for example, VKA/KVA;

- have no channels in common: "**The Scramble**," for example, AVK/VKA;

- be reversed: "**The Parentheses**," for example,
VAK/KAV.

Each combination has its own richness, its own dilemma, as the next four stories demonstrate. These people are all learning to enter another person's model of the world while maintaining their own centers of balance.

No bird soars too high if he soars with his own wings.

—Ralph Waldo Emerson

The Match: "Are We Making Love or Having a Fight?"

It's very easy to be best friends with someone whose mind uses the same pattern as yours. It's almost as if they understand things without being told. The challenge, however, is that it's also very easy for the relationship to get flat, complacent, and stuck in the same mudhole.

Justine came to a workshop entitled "Establishing Intimacy," which Andy and I taught on the East Coast. Most of the participants were there with a partner, but she sat directly across from me, with only a notebook as her companion. She scribbled furiously as I spoke. I never determined whether she wrote down the clever things I said or the infuriating ones, but she filled the better part of an entire steno pad in two sessions.

By the end of the first day, she started asking questions. Each of them began with a "but." "But what if someone hates to be touched?" "But what if someone loves the written word?" "But what if someone always talks to herself?"

Being quite familiar with the way those of us with the VAK pattern tend to ask questions that are really disguised statements, I did what I could to answer and waited until she felt safe enough to bring her real issue forward.

I didn't have long to wait. She waved her hand in my face first thing the next morning. "How does this apply to making love? My husband Fred and I have been married for 15 years. We get along quite well. We never fight. I've figured out his mind uses the same pattern as mine, VAK. We never fight. Did I say that already? The problem is we never make love either. We're real good friends and like each other well enough. We're almost like brother and sister."

She paused long enough to breathe and glance quickly around the room. There were several couples nodding and shifting uncomfortably in their seats. "I'm not turned off by Fred or anything. I'm just not turned on either. We both are so passive, lying there, thinking 'I wish she'd make the first move,' 'I wish he'd make the first move,' and we both just lie there. I've read all the sex manuals. We have three kids so we know how to do it, we just don't know how to **enjoy** doing it!"

There were several giggles in the room, but I wasn't laughing. I knew from personal experience how hard all of that must have been for Justine to talk about in this setting. For a moment my mind rubberbanded back to a time in my life when I would have loved to have asked the same question. After sharing a bit of my own history, I told her that I would like to honor her request, but since both of us had unconscious minds that were triggered by kinesthetic input, it was important that we explore her question experientially in a way that would be fun and safe. She nodded vehemently so I kept on going.

"When two people have matching patterns, it's very easy for them to slip into taking each other for granted, and it's also easy for them to get stuck in the same way.

"Telling you how you and Fred should be making love does not look, sound, or feel like fun to me. Fred didn't come to this workshop, so he doesn't get to learn this—from me. Since his mind works just like yours, and since **you** are a fine teacher ..."

As I took her hand and led her into the middle of the circle, Justine was giggling with everyone else. Until I said, "So I'm going to teach this whole group how to make love to you!"

She shrieked.

"Just for demonstration purposes, of course. You don't have to take off your clothes and no one will touch you, I promise."

The color came back into her face and she began to breathe again.

"Now group, when approaching someone whose mind uses this pattern, what is the first mode to contact?" I used my best teacher voice. Everyone responded in unison,

You have to sniff out joy. Keep your nose to the joy trail.

—Buffy Sainte-Marie (KAV)

"The conscious."

"Very good. Since that is visual for Justine, we are going to tell her how we receive her with our eyes."

I was beginning to feel like an X-rated version of Mr. Rogers, but the group was into it, and people began to call out things they saw such as "I'm looking at how the sunlight dazzles in your hair," "I'm seeing how your eyes look like chips of sky." I chimed in, "I'm noticing the little golden hairs on your cheek."

We went on like this for several minutes until her tension began to melt, her breath eased, her eyelids fluttered. "I like this a lot. It's a little awkward, but nicely awkward. Please go on, Dawna."

"We've related to your conscious mind, and apparently it's receiving us, now we'll gently ease up to your subconscious channel by turning on some soft music. What kind of music would you say is 'making-love music,' Justine?"

She shrugged. "I never thought much about it, to tell you the truth. Our stereo is in the living room. Mostly we have the television on for background noise. But it doesn't help much because my subconscious mind keeps telling me about what I should be buying the next day in the supermarket."

"The television must go in the living room and the stereo has to take its place in the bedroom. Come on, group, let's sing to Justine."

We began to croon, "You are so beautiful, you are so beautiful to me, can't you see..." As they hummed in the background, I recited poetry, softly. She sighed. And sighed again.

"Since this is for demonstration purposes only, we'll stop here." There was a chorus of groans, and Justine began to pout.

"But if we **were** to continue, we'd begin to touch your hand or your cheek while describing to you how it felt, or read to you, or breathe in your ear, murmuring so your auditory middle mind stays involved and out of the supermarket."

"Fred and I were in sex therapy for a year and we never learned stuff like this. I was supposed to initiate all the time, and I'd rub Fred's back and he'd snore and I'd give up. I felt like someone trying to jitterbug under water!"

"You **can** initiate, but you still have to respect the way both of

I'm a survivor of being taught love through techniques. Now I'm learning techniques through love.

—Jerry Cimmet,
Philadelphia, Pa.

your minds work. Send Fred notes, write love messages on the mirror, parade around in silk, take him to a candle-lit restaurant with violins. Talk about your feelings, your dreams, your sweet memories. Dance with him, slow and sexy. Can you see yourself doing any of this, Justine?"

She put her hands on her hips. Her eyes flashed, reminding me of an exclamation point looking for a place to happen. "You betcha! **This** is homework! I guess having the same pattern can become boring sometimes, but wait until I tell Fred that the whole group made love to me this weekend!"

"My professional reputation will never be the same. You are all sworn to secrecy."

The Scramble: Caught in the Middle (KVA & VAK)

When people's minds have no common symbolic language, they can bring an amazing richness to each others' lives, provoking growth on every level. The challenge of this particular combination is that sometimes it can seem as if you are with someone from another planet. It is particularly important that they are mindful of how they are affecting one another, as the following story demonstrates.

"We've been fighting about the baby a lot since she began to crawl. He tells me I don't watch her enough. I tell him he doesn't give her enough space." Margo's black-rimmed eyes snapped, and the cleft in her chin trembled. I had to shake myself a little to pay attention to her words. She was quite beautiful, meticulously made-up, tastefully dressed, and she spoke with just a trace of an accent.

"I can't help it. I see that bruise on Louise's tiny cheek and my mind keeps flashing back to the news programs on TV of all those poor, battered children. If Margo had watched her more carefully, she never would have fallen and been hurt." George crossed both arms on his chest. The muscle in his jaw jumped. He was a large, solid man, huge of heart. In the few months we had been working with this young couple, I came to know how desperately he wanted to do everything right. He had been surprised when Margo told him

---

...we sing so much of love
it's our largest industry our
most marketable product
and still we have not learned
the songs of tenderness
that might mend our
broken hearts...

—Ntozake Shange,
"Conversations with
the Ancestors,"
Riding the Moon In Texas

she was pregnant. He thought they would wait a few years until they had more money, more time for their relationship to grow. But once Louise was born, she became his obsession.

"Sometimes a child can be the meeting place of a couple's minds, the glue that holds them together. This may be particularly true since Margo's mind follows the VAK pattern and George's the KVA, leaving no specific perceptual language in common. Margo, share with me your worst fantasy of what will happen to Louise if things go on as they are.

"She'll be 42 and still sitting in her father's lap. She'll never learn to stand on her own two feet."

I asked George to do the same. "She'll be totally vulnerable, bruised, battered, neglected."

"Since Louise is too young to talk, I'd like to pretend I can speak for her. I've got three minds in me: my mother's, my father's, and my own. They're so busy with their movies that they don't even try to see me as I am. The movies they're making are about what **they** needed as babies. Mommy needed to have space so she could learn to stand on her own two feet. Daddy needed the kind of fathering that would protect him from harm. They keep giving me what **they** never got."

There was a very tenuous moment after I had spoken. I opened my eyes, and noticed Margo was weeping softly. George was trying not to notice, tapping his fingers on his biceps.

"It's true what you say," exclaimed Margo. "I was the only girl, the youngest of eight children. Everyone always carried me around, treating me as if I were an infant, even when I was 11. They called me their little doll. I was never allowed to get dirty or climb a tree or be normal."

"Inside of you, Margo, that younger self, those unmet needs to explore and to be free, still wait. If you give to Louise what you haven't given to yourself, that baby within you will resent Louise. Sometimes it's that childish self that sees red, has a temper tantrum, and **does** strike out, without even seeing who she is really hitting.

"Inside of you, George, there's also a baby who wants to be watched over, protected, held. He demands of you, Give me what you give to Louise. Feel **my** hurt, hold me when I'm scared, support

> Argue for your limitations and, sure enough, they're yours.
>
> —Richard Bach

me when I want to stand on my own two feet, be as intimate with me as you are with her. Otherwise, you're giving what I need away, even if it is to someone you love. I won't let you love her and leave me out. Protect **my** tender heart too. Encourage **me** to move towards what I want, even if I stumble and fall.'"

George's eyes were closed as I spoke. He rocked back and forth, his arms now forming a tender self-embrace.

"Most of us don't know any other way to connect besides putting our centers, our dreams, our hopes and needs, inside of another person. When he or she is not there, all we feel is a void. That's what most addiction is about. I'm not telling either of you that the best way to parent is by neglecting Louise. I **am** suggesting that the worst way is by neglecting yourselves."

George turned toward me. "I feel the truth of what you're saying. I can read every one of Louise's yeses and noes. I can read her slightest need. Yet I have no idea how to read myself." He looked at Margo. "That's what's really going on when I get so mad."

"I salute your willingness to be aware of that, George. That awareness can encapsulate your anger, so you can respond to it instead of react from it."

"Dawna, this may sound stupid, but how do we show Louise we love her if we don't see the world through her eyes? I mean, that's the only way I ever learned to mother, to live through her, the way my mother lived through me, her little doll."

I took each of their hands and walked to the corner of the room where Louise was playing with a green fuzzy dragon. "Would each of you answer that question? Tell Louise how you can love her **while** you are loving yourselves."

Margo squatted on the floor and looked directly at her daughter, whispering, "I'll let myself enjoy seeing you, taking you in with my eyes and ears. That will help me be more alert. I'll be curious about my own needs as I become more curious about yours. We can be companions in exploring how to be free and safe at the same time."

George placed one gentle hand on his wife's back, one on his daughter's blonde head. "I'll let you be a brand new spirit, unique to yourself, instead of another thing I have to do perfectly. I'll notice

And having given up life, the captain suddenly began to live.

—Carson McCullers, *Reflections In a Golden Eye*

how I read you, and learn to read my own needs as devotedly. You came from my flesh but you don't belong to me."

"What gives me courage when I listen to each of you is how you're willing to notice that what you're giving to Louise is also what you most need to be giving to yourselves. Rather than trying to control each other and Louise, you're committing to expand so you can get a sense of what's needed in the present moment."

George picked up the baby, and then reached out for Margo. He began humming in her ear and dancing the three of them around in a smooth waltz. "We always used to celebrate by dancing. My wife becomes whipped cream in my arms. This is a much better way for the baby to hold us together." Louise gurgled in a wet agreement.

The Single Point: Coming Out of the Closet (KAV & AKV)

The effect on a relationship of two patterns meeting in just the conscious mode can be that they join each other quite easily in activity, organizing, beliefs, finding meaning in the ways they reach out into the world. It may, however, be difficult for them to find resonance on a very deep level. When the single point of connection is in the unconscious mind, however, communication can be deep, almost sacred. It can also leave each person stuck in his or her own private world, as the following anecdote illustrates. It is a condensation of a session facilitated by Peggy Tileston, which she later shared with me.

The first thing Brady (KAV) did when he reached 18 was to drop out of school. Until that time, he was the ace student in all of the Vocational Training Program's carpentry courses. Building things meant everything to him. Give him a large enough pile of rough-cut two-by-fours and he'd create a new world. He'd place his hands on the wood, tilt his head to one side, as if listening to some secret deep in the grain, close his eyes to get a flash of what it wanted to be, begin to hum, and let his hands do the rest.

Fred, his father, (AKV) was living with his third wife. He was an attorney who came from a wealthy family. The most noticeable thing about Fred was his voice—loud, rough, and crusty; he loved to talk.

Our language has wisely sensed the two sides of being alone. It has created the word 'loneliness' to express the pain of being alone. And it has created the word 'solitude' to express the glory of being alone.

—Paul Tillich,
The Eternal Now

Talk is the sex of the eighties. In a time when you can hardly initiate a handshake without a note from your doctor, conversation is not just a white collar mating dance; it is the most intimate for safe sex… it is also, in the right mouths, the last civilized popular art.

—Time magazine, 7/31/89

When angry, as he was most of the time with Brady, he really bellowed. Brady referred to him as the Prosecutor.

During one joint session, Fred began his usual lecturing while Brady flopped and fidgeted in a chair. It was virtually impossible for either one of us to get a word in edgewise. Finally, Brady shot out of the chair yelling, "Screw you, Dad! You never give **me** a chance to talk!"

Fred turned to me and said, "Did you hear that? That's how my own son talks to me! He refuses to just sit still and listen. All I'm trying to do is help him, for God's sake!"

Brady was about to leave the room when I asked if he'd be willing to try an experiment. Natural curiosity overcame rage. I requested that he walk around the room while we proceeded. (All our previous successful sessions had either taken place in a car or walking.)

I complimented Fred on his facility with language, remarking that he obviously enjoyed discussions and must be frustrated when Brady clammed up or called him names. After he made a long-winded affirmative reply, I asked if he was willing to listen to Brady describe what it was like for him to converse with his dad. I also asked that he promise not to interrupt.

"I just stop hearing him after a few sentences," said Brady. "I don't know why. It's like drowning or suffocating in words. I just want him to shut up so I can breathe and think. He doesn't give **me** a chance to say anything. He just yells. I feel every word. Sometimes, I start screaming at him in my head, and then the words pour out. He says I don't listen to him, but he never listens to **me!**"

Instead of giving Fred a chance to argue, I asked him to tell me what he respected about his son. After a few sarcastic replies, he responded, "Brady's real good at making things, anything. He's a good cook, good with animals and little kids, too. He's got very competent hands. In fact, he was a big help when we lived on our farm."

I asked Brady to do the same thing. He replied slowly, "My dad's specialty is explaining things to me, when I listen. He's good with his hands, too. I know building better than he does, but he can fix most anything. And he can put on all different kinds of accents and tell jokes; he used to make me laugh a lot."

At this point, we began a mutual exploration of how their minds worked. They soon discovered their own and each other's patterns. I could see understanding begin to gleam in their eyes, as I explained why it was so important for Fred to talk things over and for Brady to do things together.

I asked Fred if he thought he could listen to Brady for five minutes without interruption. He grunted and then started to pace around the room, hands jingling the coins in his pockets.

Brady looked down at his feet, his words halting and arduous at first. Within minutes though, he was pouring out his heart to his dad, with only occasional prompting from me. At one point, he began crying, "I just want to feel that you love me, that you're trying to understand me. I want us to **do** things together. You never come riding in my car any more. That's very important to me. When I go up to you and try to hug you, you pull away. I want you to hug me back."

Knowing that father's and son's minds both met with visual input, I asked Brady to give Fred an image his father could see of how he felt in his life. "It's like that guy pushing a boulder up a hill. I'm stuck, holding it up with my back, and I don't know if I'm going to make it."

Fred was obviously moved by the vision. He related the times in his life when he had felt similarly. He also expressed how awkward and vulnerable he felt when Brady hugged him. "I just don't know what to do. My own father only touched me when he was beating me. I don't know how to be comfortable hugging anyone. I wish you wouldn't take it personally, Kiddo. I guess I **do** have a big mouth, but I don't mean anything by what I say. I haven't heard you talk so much in years. I guess conversing like this for me is what hugging is like for you."

My religion is very simple. My religion is kindness.

—Dalai Lama

Fred, Brady, and I worked out the following plan for improving their communication:

1. When Brady feels overwhelmed by Fred's words, he will hold up his hand for a few minutes of silence and space.

2. Brady can fiddle or pace when they're talking.

3. Brady will make an extra effort to find words to speak to his father. Fred will do the same to find and receive touch.

4. If they find themselves going back to the old ways of fighting, they can stop, and come up with a visual image to describe what's going on for them in that moment.

Compassion is an alternate perception.

—M.C. Richards, *Centering*

The Perceptual Parentheses: Meeting in a Closet (VAK & KAV)

When the single point that two minds meet at is in the middle, there are remarkable gifts and spectacular challenges, because these people's minds work in a completely reversed way. They are continually entrancing each other, because the most receptive aspect of one person is communicating and triggering the most active aspect of the other and vice versa. What is sacred to one is casual to the other. Understanding this and being able to find each other in the middle meeting place is essential, as the following story illustrates.

When Andy and I were building our home, each trip I made to the supermarket meant buying another house magazine. There were piles of *Home, House Beautiful, Kitchens and Bathroom Design, Architect's Digest,* and *Women's Day Decorating* in every corner of our rental place.

True to the VAK pattern of my natural intelligence, each morning, I casually went through every one, cutting out photographs of rooms I loved, colors I had to live in, carpets, rocking chairs, lighting fixtures, appliances, and arched windows. I then carefully filed everything in a bulging accordion-type orange folder. This made the house more of a reality to me, and I felt as though I were contributing something important.

Each night when Andy would come home from digging the foundation, I'd cuddle up to him, take my visionary display from its folder and babble on about the possibilities I saw. He'd put one arm around my shoulder, nod, and as I went on discussing the newest plans, close his eyes and begin to snorfle—not exactly indications of the alert interest I was looking for. He was not only tired from a day of heavy labor, my natural "show and tell" was triggering him into KAV theta land quicker than a sleeping pill.

There followed several disagreements; let me be more explicit—there were many fights over the construction of the new house. Each time I'd want to plan what was going to go where, each time I'd shake a page of blueprint or yellow tissue paper in his face, Andy would get pale and begin to pace. I'd stomp around the room asking him how we could build a house without plans.

To which he would reply, "Simple, I'll just **do** it and then we'll step back and see what we've got and go from there."

I did not understand. I just could not conceive of how anyone could build an entire house without a single plan. He **did** write things down, though. As the walls went up, I found little pieces of wood scraps with penciled numbers, or simple line drawings of a joist here, an arch there.

One day, several months later, I decided to take a surprise visit to Andy and our crew of three, whom we had fondly named "The Studly Stallions." Jeff and Brady were 19-year-old friends of David, my son. (I privately called them the Testosterone Trio. Lord knows what they privately called **me!)**

I entered our new front door, turned to my right and smiled as I saw the newly finished kitchen. Turning to my left, I saw … a closet … blocking the way. How had that closet gotten there? There was supposed to be a long expanse of floor there, leading to the big window in the living room, so I could stand at the sink washing dishes and see the sun set. We hadn't planned on putting any closet there to block my view or cut in half what *Women's Day* magazine called "The Great Room."

I shrieked. Andy was installing wiring in the closet wall and dropped his electric screwdriver. He calmly explained that we needed someplace to put our boots and wet coats when we came in during the winter, and it seemed natural to put it there right by the door.

"But we didn't **plan** it!" I wailed. "My dishwashing view is ruined. It's not supposed to **look** like this."

"Look, shmook, it's the only way it **works,** Dawna. And I've

> Melnick says the soul is immortal and lives on after the body drops away, but if my soul exists without my body, I am convinced all my clothes will be loose fitting.
>
> —Woody Allen,
> *Without Feathers*

spent all day building it and wiring it and it's not coming down."

"But if only you would have drawn it on paper **first,** we could have just erased it. You can't erase wood."

The Studly Stallions quietly slipped off their ladders and out of the front door as our voices rose in volume. Every skill in conflict resolution we both knew and taught followed them. I completely forgot about how Andy's mind works exactly the opposite of mine. I never even considered that a brain like his does not plan in the same way as mine does. I didn't want to consider anything except my view. We shouted, screamed, snarled, cajoled, convinced, complained, cried, and finally compromised.

Andy tore out the top half of the closet, since it had no wiring in it. I could see my view, and he had a half closet for his muddy boots. If anyone asked what it was, and several people did, David would declare, "Oh, that's where their minds meet."

Understanding how your mind and another's process information will not guarantee you'll live happily ever after. But hopefully, it **will** give you just enough new information to cause you pause at the "sizzle points" in inquiry instead of confrontation. The word "respect," at its root, means to see again. Hopefully, it will bring you to a new respect for both yourself and the other person. Hopefully, it can help you remember to ask, "How can I be available to myself and my needs, while simultaneously being available to reach out in curiosity to others?"

Alert, waking consciousness, your ordinary state, your cultural trance, is when we all dream the same dream, more or less, and call it Reality.

—Robert Masters & Jean Houston, *Mind Games*

CHAPTER 13

LIVING IN THE QUESTIONS

*The wider your understanding of human
nature, the biological processes, the history of individual living, the wider your
knowledge of your own reactions, of your
own potentials, the better you will practice and the better you will live.*

—Milton Erickson

What follows are some of the questions people ask most frequently as
they are learning to understand and integrate this material. You may recognize
your own uncertainties here. My responses are not the definitive or final
"answer" to these questions. They are the best I can do to honor the
inquiry by bringing my experience and curiosity to it.

Dialogue with Frequently Asked Questions

Q: Does my pattern change throughout my life? Are we born or made this way?

A: I'm really not sure if we are born with perceptual preferences. Some infants seem to have an extremely strong leaning toward one pattern or another. Others don't. Overall, I believe most of us are shaped into these patterns by our social environment. If a mother's mind uses the auditory channel to consciously organize her experience, and a father's uses kinesthetic, if their son wants to be like his daddy, it would be logical that his brain might learn to match that same perceptual language. A child from an alcoholic family, where everyone in the house is denying or numbing out emotions, may become smart kinesthetically so he or she can feel and do for the whole family.

These patterns are thinking pathways. They can change, particularly the front two channels, but they usually get habitually grooved in by adolescence.

My son's conscious mind mode changed its language when he went through puberty. I've known people to rearrange patterns as a side effect of a variety of profound life-altering situations. If a child experiences a lot of abuse in one channel, for instance, he or she may push that as far away from consciousness as possible in order not to have to "think" about the abuse.

Q: What if you are blind or deaf or physically challenged? How does that affect your perceptual pattern?

A: There's no set answer. In my experience, some people, when blind, still form visual images that are quite clear to them. Others don't. It's important to understand that when we're talking about visual or auditory or kinesthetic, we're not speaking of acuity, but rather about thought and imagery—inner vision, voices and feelings.

Q: Why can't someone be an AKA? Why can't they be in the beta and theta modes of their mind at the same time?

A: The modes are triggered one by one, much in the way that

> Religion is not any particular teaching. Religion is everywhere.
>
> —Suzuki Roshi

dominoes fall. It's just doesn't seem possible to be conscious and unconscious at the same time. Which is a good way to check on your pattern because it is very difficult for a person to function from their beta mode and theta mode simultaneously. People whose minds use the VAK pattern, for instance, have to close their eyes to know what they are feeling in their body. Conversely, if they're being touched, writing becomes much more difficult. Talking, for someone whose mind uses the AVK pattern, blocks their feeling and is difficult while they are walking. When someone who is word smart and visually sensitive begins to read, they stop talking. A body-smart and word-sensitive pattern stops moving to listen deeply. The middle mind blocks or enhances this connection, so that hand motions help VKAs find words, writing helps KVAs or AVKs describe what they are feeling, and talking about what they're feeling helps KAVs find their inner dreams and visions.

Q: It seems I'm visually smart. How can I be sure?

A: Look at me for as long as is comfortable for you.

Q: I can do that forever. Why?

A: If you sorted visually, you'd be able to maintain eye contact comfortably for a while, but relatively soon, especially if you wanted to speak or move, you'd have to look away. If your unconscious mind was triggered visually, it would be very difficult to hold eye contact for even a minute or two.

Q: Then how come I'm always asking other people to look for the things I've lost?

A: It is your most stimulated channel; because of that, you may not have such great visual discrimination. Since you use your eyes so much, it's as if they get calloused and stop noticing things with great receptivity.

Q: I understand how the different minds use words differently, but it's hard for me to really understand how we see things differently? Also how is kinesthetic different for the different mind?

A: One of the most difficult things about this approach to understanding how we think is the realization that other people may

> Develop your own technique. Don't try to use somebody else's technique… Don't try to imitate my voice or cadence. Just discover your own. Be your own natural self. It's the individual responding to the individual.
>
> —Milton Erickson

actually not perceive the world the way we do. On one level, that is obvious, but on a deeper level, that awareness shatters some of the most basic assumptions we carry. A friend whose theta mind is visually triggered pointed out to me that an associate just couldn't see how his behavior was affecting everyone else at work. "Why can't he just step back and see the whole picture and then change?" he insisted.

Consequently, I asked two excellent photographers, Larry Rippel and Rachel Edwards, who have been exploring this approach for quite some time, to imagine they were a camera being held in the hands of three people of different perceptual persuasions—one whose beta mind is triggered by visual input into concentrating, one whose alpha mind is triggered by visual input into sorting, and one whose theta mind is triggered by visual input into generating—to take pictures of the same scene from each perspective. The two sets of photographs that resulted from this experiment can be found on the pages that follow.

It is important to note that none of us have a weak or nonexistent functioning in any of the different modes. Each mental instrument responds to input in very different ways. Mary Pat Mengato, a dancer and movement therapist, describes the kinesthetic differences in the different patterns:

KVA & KAV: Their movements tend to be big, loose, easy, natural. They seem as if clothes are just meant to comfort them. Compared to the other patterns, they can move and stay active for a very long time without getting tired. They don't think before they move, they just let their bodies lead them. The faster they move, the faster they think. Their sense of space and physical environment is immediate and very relevant to their functioning.

VKA & AKV: They can be still, but their hands are very mobile. If they're paying attention to the outer world, they're physically quite active, but as they notice their own sensations and feelings, their movement slows. Touching another sometimes makes it difficult for them to know what they are feeling in their own bodies.

VAK & AVK: Whatever is going on in their conscious minds (showing, reading, or talking) can totally block their movement or

The moment we cease to hold each other, the moment we break faith with one another, the sea engulfs us and the light goes out.

—James Baldwin

feeling. What's going on in the middle (listening or watching) can enhance it. They move almost as if it's for the first time. Somehow, they don't seem to "fit" with ease into their bodies. If they close down their conscious minds and really allow themselves to go deep inside, their movements seem otherworldly, sacred, fragile and very personal. Being touched is sometimes experienced as "interfering with their concentration."

Q: What is the effect of various drugs on all of this?

A: I can only speak with some certainty of my own experience with three common drugs—alcohol, marijuana, and cocaine. Alcohol affects people's kinesthetic capacities first, their ability to feel, to move and to coordinate; it then, in a domino effect, incapacitates their minds from conscious to unconscious modes.

I was addicted to marijuana for 20 years, and have worked with hundreds of people who have used and abused it. As far as we can tell, marijuana causes the conscious mind to function but not record. It is like a tape recorder or video camera that operates, but has no tape in it. You have an experience, it goes right through your beta mode without leaving an impression, and gets processed in the alpha and theta modes.

Thus, you cannot separate out or discriminate between what is good or bad—a function of the conscious mind. That's why stoned ideas all seem to be of genius quality to the person thinking them.

When stoned on marijuana, I found myself extraordinarily lazy, although at the time I would have said I was just going with the flow. The experiences I did have while stoned are quite difficult to access. I have a very strong visual memory, yet when trying to recall any book I read during those 20 years, I cannot see the title or the page as I can with books I read before and after. I remember the feelings and most of the verbal content, but getting there takes me a while. It's like sticking my hand under water to fumble around for a coin dropped in a stream.

What marijuana did do was enable me to get past the criticisms and judgments of my conscious mind long enough to experience fully some of my moments and create from them. I loved being alone when stoned. I could lie on my back and become the faces I saw in

Each person is an individual. Hence, psychotherapy should be formulated to meet the uniqueness of the individual's needs, rather than tailoring the person to fit the Procrustean bed of a hypothetical theory of human behavior.

—Milton Erickson

visual beta

visual alpha

visual theta

visual beta

visual alpha

visual theta

the knotholes of the pine boards on our ceiling without my conscious mind's reminding me of all the things I needed to do.

It is my belief that marijuana gave a whole generation of us the unedited experience of our alpha and theta consciousnesses. Unfortunately, we could never use those experiences to effect any lasting change. That may explain the pendulum swing in the other direction now, to learn the missing skills necessary to live out our dreams.

Which brings me to cocaine, the pharmacological parenthesis of marijuana, since it forces a person to function mostly in beta mode. Consequently, when using cocaine, a person gets quite linear, active, and self-serving. It is virtually impossible for people doing cocaine to connect with anyone or anything else on a deep level. They become walking left brains. It does help them "get ahead," temporarily, by "living in the fast lane." It also makes it possible to kill or abuse others by making them seem mere objects.

Q: In your opinion, how does one achieve intimacy?

A: The process, from this approach's perspective, consists of receiving oneself and/or another through the perceptual channels of one's conscious, subconscious, and unconscious mind.

Q(AVK): All I know about how my mind operates is that I'm word smart, as you would say. But I do notice that all these people with kinesthetic triangle minds can sit around and cuddle so casually. I'm the opposite. I am not comfortable doing that. Is there something wrong with me?

A: No. Your brain is a different kind of instrument, that's all. To people whose conscious minds are kinesthetically triggered, cuddling is like chitchat would be to you. When **you** cuddle, you take someone all the way into your unconscious mind. So you need to know that person very well, have lots of good talks, then silence, then a shared visual image of some kind, or eye contact at a slow rhythm, and finally The Cuddle.

Q(AVK): I need to know how I can communicate with these

It is no use walking anywhere to preach unless our walking is our preaching.

—St. Francis Of Assisi

people whose sensitive minds are triggered by words. Why shouldn't I give them answers to their questions? You don't hesitate to answer those of us that are word smart.

A: Good question. It's probably better to wait to answer yours as well, because AVKs and AKVs usually answer their own questions very shortly after they ask them. You have a wonderful ability to define things in a linear way. A good philosophical discussion to you is like a stretching warm-up is to a KVA or KAV.

For people whose unconscious minds are triggered by words, questions are a turning of the compass, as if they were saying, "I wonder which way I need to go to find home?" If you answer for them, it would be like taking the compass out of their hands and pointing in the direction of **your** house.

Q(AVK): How would you find out what someone's perceptual pattern is through casual conversation?

A: Begin by letting your ears get receptive, and your eyes get soft, as if you're inhaling through your pupils. As you speak, include one channel's images, for instance, "It's like a hand grabbing tofu." If the response is slow, if the person looks blank, it's possible that his or her unconscious mind processes information kinesthetically. (It's also possible the person doesn't know what tofu is or they only speak Portuguese.) Try another kind of image. "Well, you see, it's like trying to figure out what to write in the blank spaces on your income tax form." Keep switching modes until you can tell which is the most resounding, alert response, when he or she says "Yeah! Yeah!," and which is the monotone "duh."

Q(AVK): I want a simple way to remember what I've read. I go blank sometimes.

A: Use your dominant hand to write the question you want answered, and allow your non-dominant hand to write a reply. It will access farther back in your mind than your habitual hand will. The handwriting may not be pretty, but what one hand forgets, the other may remember. I'm sure you've heard yourself say, "On the one

We've kept our pain inside. When you do that, you don't feel other people's pain. The only way to learn compassion is through your heart; you have to back up and pass through your own pain.

—Matthew Fox, as quoted in *Common Boundary*, July/August 1980

hand ... but on the other hand ..."

Everything you've learned and experienced is stored in your unconscious mind, even if you're not aware of it. Everything that's been dropped into the ocean eventually comes to rest on the bottom, even if we can't tell it's there from the surface. "Remembering" merely means finding a way to bring it to the surface. If you tell yourself, "I'll never remember this," your brain accepts that the way a computer accepts a command to delete information.

For those whose conscious or subconscious minds are visually triggered, writing with the non-dominant hand can float things forward. You can, of course, use the same process to answer other questions you have about decisions you're trying to make, personal history that's been forgotten, advice on your creative process. But don't expect it to give you linear answers, any more than you'd expect a map to tell you why Toledo is where it is.

Many people are willing to spend a great deal of time and energy traveling to gurus and teachers outside themselves, but they completely ignore their own inner wisdom. Please treat whatever is revealed by your other hand with the same respect you would advice from a revered external teacher.

Q(AKV): I'm really interested in using affirmations. They are quite satisfying, but unfortunately I don't really think they have a very profound effect on me. Could you comment on different forms of self-healing?

A: There was a time in my life when I was quite ill, and visualization was the new cure-all. Every morning and night, I visualized the bad cells being eaten by the good cells. That affected my conscious visual channel only. But it was my **unconscious** kinesthetic channel that influenced my immune system. The movie alone did not get back there. When I added a story to it and acted it out with my hands, moved it or sculpted it, all three channels became involved, and ultimately I felt the effects of the story in my body.

Q: My mind uses the AKV pattern. How come I don't seem to ever hang out with other AKVs very much?

Let the beauty we love be what we do.

—Rumi

A: Most AKVs love to inspire others and thus need to be received to be listened to, to move others, to be seen. In other words, they need to be received. So one AKV trying to inspire another AKV who is trying to inspire...

Q(VAK): Since my conscious mind is visually triggered, does that mean I need to write to people in order to communicate in a linear way?

A: Your written communication may, in fact, be more logical. In order to communicate "from your heart," try to feel what it is that needs saying in you, and translate that into spoken words that paint images.

Q(VAK): I'd like some way to communicate with the signals my body sends me. I have a headache right now, for instance. What is that trying to tell me? Should I take an aspirin or what?

A: It's possible to "read" body messages by using them as a kind of biofeedback mechanism. You begin by establishing a "yes" signal. Just ask your unconscious how it will indicate yes to you.

Q: The throbbing in my head got more intense.

A: Fine. Now ask it how it will signal "no."

Q: That's weird... the throbbing diminished noticeably.

A: Good. Now ask it how it will respond "neither."

Q: All sensation disappeared, as if I had Novocain.

A: OK. Now ask any question that you're really curious about, making sure it can be answered by a simple yes or no. Ask with genuine curiosity.

Q: Amazing! It worked. I asked if I should take aspirin and the feeling diminished: that means no. But when I asked if there was something else it needed, it got intense, meaning yes. When I asked if I was making all of this up, it signaled no again. Fascinating. How do I find out what it needs?

A: Just keep checking out all of the possibilities that pop into your mind, one by one. (An important caveat: This process is NOT meant to take the place of medical doctors or diagnostic testing. But it **can** help you discover what you can do on your own to maximize

I am done with great things and big plans, great institutions and big success. I am for those tiny, invisible loving human forces that work from individual to individual, creeping through the crannies of the world like so many rootlets, or like the capillary oozing of water, yet which, if given time, will rend the hardest monuments of human pride.

—William James

the effectiveness of standard medical treatment.)

Q: My mind uses the VKA pattern. How do I filter what comes in?

A: We live in a very verbal time. I call it the Age of the Mouth. The late sixties and early seventies were much more kinesthetic, as evidenced by statements like "Make love, not war," and "Go with the flow"; by the popularity of "Sensitivity groups" to help explore feelings; and the interest in the body/mind connection.

My work is me. It is for this I have come.

—Gerard Manley Hopkins

These days it's self-improvement lectures to discuss how you can get ahead, make more money, etc. For auditorily sensitive minds, this can be very assaultive, because the main mode of communication—words—is always going directly into your unconscious mind. It would be the same as if any time you came into contact with someone you had to get naked immediately.

The middle mind, in your case the kinesthetically subconscious mode, tries to protect your unconscious. Frequently the only way it knows how to do that is for your body to protest. But in time, the mechanism of this protective solution becomes the mechanism of the problem—a disease or a physical breakdown that forces you to withdraw from further contact. It is trying to filter, the only way it knows how. What the VKA mind pattern really needs most is silence and recharging.

Recharging means turning your mind inward. While reading, listening to the radio, watching TV, or running may relax and entertain your conscious mind, keeping it occupied, they do not give you the opportunity to connect with your supply lines. Just as when you drive a car, eventually you need to stop and get your tank filled.

Q(VKA): I have been in excruciating pain a lot this last week. My husband is AVK, and he won't talk about his feelings. I notice when he's not in the house, I'm fine, but the minute he walks in I hurt in my body. If I get a headache and ask him what he's feeling in his body, he says his head hurts. My father was an alcoholic and the same thing happened with him. If my husband talks about what's going on for him, I don't feel it any more. He rarely listens to me, by the way. He just keeps saying, "Get to the point!"

A: As you talk, I notice your hands keep gesturing with a pen, and moving as if you're writing. Why don't you carry a little pad around with you, and write notes about what you are feeling in your body, wherever it's coming from. You'll be carrying your feelings into your conscious mind, and be less receptive to his. Writing will do for you what talking does for him.

Also, since he's asking you to get to the point, writing will help your mind condense its thinking. Write to yourself when you're around him, so if there's something he won't listen to, you can make sure it's received by you.

Q(VKA): I have always thought there was something wrong with me because I felt everyone else's pain. But I don't have to touch someone else to do it: I just look at the person, and then, sometimes without realizing, I seem to feel what he or she is feeling—in my body. Weird, huh?

A: I worked with a woman several years ago, let's call her Susie, whose mind used the VKA pattern just like yours. We sat across from each other on cushions. One day I was wearing a purple angora sweater. Susie was wearing a white v-necked cotton T-shirt. For the first hour of our session, she kept scratching and scratching at her neck. I finally asked her if she was allergic to angora. She answered that she was indeed and seemed quite shocked I knew.

In fact, she was feeling what she saw, particularly because she was sitting still and staring. People sometimes refer to "getting sucked into" someone else's problem. What we have been talking about is the mechanism of that phrase.

Q(VKA): I'm confused. I'm accused of constantly talking, yet my unconscious mind uses the auditory channel. How come I'm not the silent type?

A: "Pinwheel" talking may be the only way you learned to protect your sacred ears from all the words that come at them. When you talk incessantly, you're saying what you once heard said to you, since your unconscious mind can be like a tomb for words. The

Turn your face to the sun and the shadows fall behind you.

—Maori proverb

words that come out may have a linear tone of voice, but usually they go around in circles rather than nice, neat, linear explanations. It's like protective coloration in an animal.

Q: That **is** true. When I talk that way, no one really seems to understand me. It doesn't happen when I ask questions, though. I'm very good at asking questions, and I can go on with that for hours too—**they** feel as if they're mine.

A: That's one of your strengths. Many excellent doctors' and therapists' minds use a VKA pattern for that very reason. This strength has its weakness, however, since you're sharing your most private mind with the outside world. You need someone to receive you, to ask you questions, instead of filling in words for you. If you don't get that, you may find yourself jabbering again.

Isn't it amazing how your brain will protect you, no matter what, as well as doing whatever is necessary to help you meet your needs?

Q(KVA): My four-year-old daughter's mind uses the AVK pattern. She shouts at me frequently. She is always pulling on me, whining, "Listen to me, Mommy," until I see red and whack her. Then I feel terribly guilty. I just feel like I can't get any space. What do you suggest?

A: Take a few days to play a new game with her. Teach her how to make her voice different sizes: little enough to fit in a tiny jewel box; big enough to fit in an empty shoe box; big enough to fill the bathroom, but not leak out into the living room; big enough to fill the car; big enough to fill the whole outdoors. Overdo it. Then teach her how big her loving voice should be to fit into a magical ear. Have her teach you the size touch that is big enough for the whole outdoors; for a big adult man; for a tiny baby; and how big a loving touch should be to fit a child's magical skin.

Q(KVA): This may seem like a strange question, but it's really important to me. It's about my basketball coach. I don't understand a word she says. She shouts instructions at me and I just space out. It's at its worst before a game when she rattles off directions. The next thing I know she's clapping her hands, and I don't have the vaguest

A knowledge of the path cannot be substituted for putting one foot in front of the other.

—M.C. Richards, *Centering*

idea what she's said. I feel retarded.

A: Your coach's mind probably uses the AKV pattern. Her way of using language would trigger your unconscious mind, which makes it very difficult for you to stay alert when she talks. Before the game, stand next to her instead of across from her and take notes while she speaks. If she speaks too fast, put your hand on her shoulder while she's talking to slow her down enough so you can catch up with her words.

Q(KVA): I guess I need some reassurance. Does this mean there are certain things I can't do even if I want to because of my learning pattern?

A: Please come over here next to me. Now face that chair where you were just sitting in. Imagine you can see yourself still there. Please give that self the reassurance she needs. You know her much better than I do, so I'm sure you'll do a better job.

Q: I'll try. "You … can … do … do whatever … you want." It's really hard, Dawna.

A: OK. Let's go to your subconscious mind. Here's some paper and a pen. Write that self a message of reassurance.

Q: (After writing furiously for several minutes) That was much easier. It just flowed out.

A: "You **can** do whatever you want." Just think of yourself as a fine instrument. If Pablo Casals were standing in the middle of Grand Central Station trying to play a Mozart etude while hundreds of people were pushing and shouting all around him, he'd have a very difficult time. That doesn't mean there's anything wrong with Casals or his cello. Casual chitchat, a telephone, a bar is like Grand Central Station for your mind. Do you see that?

Q: I really do. No wonder I've always hated cocktail parties. I thought it was because I was just shy or introverted.

Q(KVA): I've spent years trying to find myself in therapy and I've learned to be quite happy alone—writing, doing photography, walking in the woods. But now I want more. I want connection, intimacy with another person, and I'm terrified I'll find "the other," but

There is a life force, an energy, a quickness that is translated through you into action. If you block it, the world will not have it. You do not have to believe in yourself or your work. It is not your business to compare yourself with others. It is your business to keep open and aware directly to the urges that motivate you, to keep the channel open.

—Martha Graham

lose me. Do you have any suggestions?

A: We seem to live in a binary age of either/or. If your unconscious mind is for you, and your conscious mind is for "other," then your subconscious mind is for balancing both. In your case, in order to find intimacy ("in-to-me-see"), you need to process what you feel about the other by looking away or down or closing your eyes. If you make eye contact steadily, you'll find "in-to-them-see," being able only to think about what **they** want, what **they** think, what **they** feel. That visual sorting mode of yours is like a revolving glass door. You need to use it to go in as well as to go out. That may mean writing about how you're feeling or painting or taking photographs or even doing mathematical equations on a blackboard.

Q(KVA): My mother keeps complaining about me. I've just bought a car. Now I'm sitting down to do a budget and figure out how to pay for it. She thinks this is irresponsible, and that I should have figured my budget out first. What do you think?

A: You're both right. For the way her brain works (which probably is visually smart), she would have to **see** it in black and white before she does it. But for your brain . . .

Q: I have to **do** it, and then see how I'm going to pay for it! Far out!

Q: My mind uses the KVA pattern and I tend to get in close relationships only with other KVAs. Why?

A: A friend of mine, whose mind uses this channel, says that when it comes to intimate relationships, KVAs are "homoceptuals." They find it easiest to get their needs for solitude and quiet, measured rhythm, and understanding of how to do things systematically from other KVAs.

Q(KVA): One day recently, I was watching the Oprah Winfrey show. Her guest was a famous advice columnist, and the panel consisted of couples who were all having difficulties in their marriages. Her advice to all of them could be summed up as "Talk to each other more. Talk, talk, talk. Forget about doing anything else, just talk.

The opposite of talking isn't listening. The opposite of talking is waiting.

—Fran Lebowitz

Lying down or standing up, you have to talk to each other. Communication is everything and if you can't talk to each other, you'll never get along. Do you hear what I'm saying? If he won't talk about what he's feeling, tell him he has to go to a counselor with you and learn to talk about what he's feeling. I hear these problems all the time, and I know what I'm talking about." I was stunned into thinking there was something really wrong with me, Dawna, because talking is the hardest thing I have to do in my life. My partner and I hardly ever talk. Our main mode of communication is e-mail. I thought we were getting along just fine, but now I'm not so sure. What do you think?

A: Talk, talk, talk, may be just the solution for someone whose mind follows the same pattern as the advice columnist's (AVK). But for someone like you, it might actually cause problems. Perhaps what you need is to show, show, show, or do, do, do in order to communicate skillfully. And perhaps all you need to do is study what's already working for you, and encourage yourself to follow in your own footsteps.

Q(KAV): I used to be called a "scatterbrain," but since I've been studying karate, I have a much easier time concentrating. Why?

A: When they called you a scatterbrain in school, you were spending most of your time in your alpha and theta modes—writing, reading, talking, listening. Since your brain uses the kinesthetic channel to concentrate...

Q: I've got it! Since I've been hanging out in the gym instead of the classroom, and since I've been working as a carpenter, I'm giving my logical mind a workout. Maybe I should go back to school to relax a little bit. I've been like a nonstop dynamo!

Q(KAV): I've noticed that when I'm speaking to someone else and I close my eyes or look away, my words sound more like me than when my eyes are open. Do you know what I mean? Why is that?

A: If your eyes are open and you're looking at someone else, your theta mind is getting continual input from the outside world, which you receive, connect with, and eventually drift off into. It's as if you were a toothpaste tube with a hole in the bottom. With your eyes

Looking for God is like seeking a path in a field of snow; if there is no path and you are looking for one, walk across it and there is your path.

—Thomas Merton

closed or looking away, your mind can draw words from your own images.

CHAPTER 14

RISK YOUR SIGNIFICANCE

I
will
not die
an unlived life
I will not live in fear
of falling or catching fire.
I choose to inhabit my days,
to allow my living to open me,
to make me less afraid, more accessible,
to loosen my heart until it becomes a wing, a torch,
a promise.
I choose
to risk my significance;
to live so that which came to me
as seed goes to the next as blossom,
and that which came to me as blossom
goes on as fruit.

—D.M.

The Challenge to Risk Your Significance

Sensei Kuboyama glides over to each member of the Ki-Aikido class, gently pushing our chests or backs, pulling our arms or ankles to determine if we are balanced. At first I thought he was testing, like most of the other teachers I have had—playing "Hah, hah I caught you off center!" But that thought dissolves as soon as I experience how supportively he stays present with each of us, challenging persistently, tenderly until we find our centers of gravity. Inevitably, he then smiles, says "Ah that's how!" and goes on.

It took me only a few classes to realize I had no idea whether I was centered or not until the sensei challenged me with that gentle push. One Tuesday night, he stated quietly, "Like in life, yes? The challenges that life brings help us to know whether we have lost our one point of balance. If so, we have only to come back to center."

This last chapter is such a challenge. It is not a test to determine whether you have learned what your perceptual pattern is or if you know how to communicate compassionately with someone of another perceptual persuasion. It is a challenge to discover if there are places in your own life where you could use what you have learned in this book to come into balance. It is also a challenge to risk your significance.

Using This Ethically: In Clean Hands

Everyone hates being categorized. All of us hate thinking that someone else knows more about us than we do. We've all had the experience of being explained **to** ourselves in ways that have been damaging, wounding: "You're not really very creative, dear, why don't you try baseball?" "I've taught for years and I know you're tone deaf, so just accept that." Those expert explanations of our capacities become limitations, corsets laced so tightly around our minds that we cannot breathe or move freely. When it comes to the workings of the human mind, we are all apprentices.

I once sat in a day-long meditation retreat with a colored dot on my forehead. The *roshi* (teacher) had put a different one on each person. There were no mirrors. We were to sit completely silent or walk

It appears that even the different parts of the same person do not converse among themselves, do not succeed in learning from each other what are their desires and intentions.

—Rebecca West

in a prescribed way, our hands folded, concentrating on our breath.

It didn't take me long to realize that everyone in the room knew the color of my dot. Everyone except me. I also knew something about them that they themselves did not. The thought passed through my meditating mind to cheat silently and mouth "red" as the tall man from Boston calmly walked by, or "blue" to the woman from Detroit who sat on the other side of the room. But I had committed myself to this learning and I knew that, like a riddle, it held a mystery. (Besides, no one else appeared to be defiant enough to cheat **with** me!)

As the day wore on, I came to realize that it was quite natural to want to know, and quite familiar not to. How much it was like my life. I had gone to therapists and teachers to help me discover how I should live, but even if they had told me directly, I would have had to search anyway. If they had pointed and said, "See? See your path? See what you're supposed to be doing?" Would it really have been useful? If they made the voyage ahead of me, telling me exactly what to do, I would still have to climb on the raft myself and struggle to make the journey.

If you use the information you have gathered from this book to categorize other people, you are not using it in clean hands. If you use it to tell people who they are and how they should live, you are not using it in clean hands.

When I teach people, they should not leave thinking **I** am brilliant; they should leave thinking **they** are brilliant. Too many people who serve as therapists and teachers use their expertise as power **over** other people. They do therapy or teach **to** instead of **with.**

The information you have received in this book can be used as a tool or as a weapon. It can prevent intimacy or foster it. It can be used to differentiate people into categories of red dots and blue dots and yellow dots, to rank and separate, or it can be used to connect us one with the other in an exquisite tapestry of hue and texture.

This book is a raft, not the river. It offers a tool, and the skills to use it, not answers. Communicating and relating are an art form. I can learn the skills that will help me use a word processor. But that

God is love, but get it in writing.
—Gypsy Rose Lee

does not mean I can write. The art involves using the skills and the tools to express the richness of my life.

Using this information in clean hands means choosing to be with another in wonder and respect: "I wonder how he is thinking that. I wonder what it would be like to perceive the world the way she does. I wonder how someone's mind would have to work to be able to do that well. I wonder how I could communicate this in a way she could receive it. I wonder how I can get through to him."

Using this information in clean hands means being willing to know others through your heart as well as through your brain; being willing to walk in their shoes, see the world through their eyes, speak their languages.

Using this information in clean hands means being willing never to know anything about another person for sure, and being quite comfortable with that. "I thought walking together would bring us closer, but he seems more uptight; let me try writing him a note." For ten years, I was absolutely sure that my friend Joanne's mind used the same pattern as mine. I told her, and since I was so sure, we both functioned as if that were true. Unfortunately, a decade later, we both realized I was terribly mistaken. Ever since, even when I am absolutely sure I understand how someone's mind works, a little part of mine stands back, whispering "Maybe, but I wonder if...." The gift from this big mistake has been that each of us has learned to walk side by side with this approach, rather than obediently behind it.

Have you ever run your fingers over a page of braille? Imagine what it would be like to have hands so curious, so observant, so exquisitely receptive to each little dot that your fingers and mind together could read them? Those are clean hands. If you can conceive of them, you can create them.

When I worked with children in a classroom, I found it much more effective to ask them to originate the rules than for me to impose mine on them. In deciding that I wanted to train other people to use this approach in their work, I chose to do what I had done in the classroom rather than try to legislate a code of ethics. One of the requisites for certification is a statement from the applicant on what he or she considers the "rules" of using this system to be. The following distillation was submitted by a New Hampshire minister.

From Rev. Marjean Bailey to Rev. Marjean Bailey

1. Don't use this with individuals or a group without their knowledge and approval of what you are doing.

2. Give credit to your teachers.

3. If you want to experiment, ask for permission and give the person room to stop at any time s/he asks to.

4. Respect the contribution of each person and seek to find his or her beauty.

5. Go as slowly as necessary so as not to violate either the individual's or the group's soul, and yet try to be courageous enough to speak the truth when necessary, intervening with care, and be willing to acknowledge your mistakes.

6. Use as many presentation modes as possible in preaching, teaching, healing and community building, so everyone will feel included.

7. Honor joy as well as pain.

8. Do not manipulate a member of the group by what you know about how that person's mind works in order to serve some intention you are holding.

> How do I work? I grope.
>
> —Albert Einstein

Applying Your Learnings:
The Challenge to Become a Bridge

On the fifth day of a conference I attended in the spring several years ago, outside Washington, D.C., Thich Nhat Hanh, a Vietnamese Buddhist monk, told a story about the difference between transmission and transformation. He described how we pass on mutated seeds of violence, destruction, and fear from generation to generation. "Each of us also has the option to transform those seeds; to create a dome of warmth, a greenhouse of peace; to water the seeds with our tears and fertilize them with our wisdom. Then, what we pass on will be transformed into something live and whole."

As he spoke, I was acutely aware that we sat just a few miles from the troubled Washington suburb of Anacostia, where more children are killed in one month than in a year in Belfast, Northern Ireland. How do we create that dome of warmth? How do we build that greenhouse of peace and safety?

How do I curve this model back to its source, like a snake whose tail is in its mouth? How do I bring it to Jerome's sisters in the migrant labor camps of Florida, to Detroit, to the children having children in Four Corners, whose tiny wombs hold their only chance for love?

What about Anacostia? Whenever I have been exposed to a new psychological or educational methodology, I ask, "But what about Anacostia? Will it make a difference there? Will it help there?" It's not that I think Anacostia is necessarily more important than Damariscotta, Maine. It's just that we need to remember our whole human tribe.

I don't think we can afford to go on pretending that an immense part of our population is not in need of support, resources, education. By finding out how we can teach the children of Anacostia more effectively, we may also find a way to improve how we teach the children in Damariscotta.

Sister Agnes taught me years ago that there are two kinds of ignorance: vincible and invincible. The former is blameless, since it originates from a lack of exposure to knowledge. But the latter is an ignorance that is willed, a conscious turning away from the truth, a denial of it. You have read this book, I have written it. Thus both of us are now responsible for finding a way of embedding whatever it offers, whatever we perceive as useful, into the institutions of this culture that are designed to teach, to serve, and to heal.

There are few of us who do not know that the distribution of resources in this society, including educational resources, is becoming severely out of balance. One of the reasons I wrote this book was out of the frustration of only teaching "them that has." I am not asking you or myself to deprive ourselves, merely to pass on our fullness to others.

There's nowhere you can go and only be with people who are like you.

—Bernice Johnson Reagon

Though I don't like to admit it, there was a point, years ago, when I was hoarding my mind. While training psychotherapists and teachers, I was secretly afraid that if I taught everything I knew, I would be out of work, discarded, extinct. I doled out what I taught: so much this year, then let them come back another year if they want more. I cringe as I write this, but it is true. This hoarding of my mind was a spiritual sickness.

My life has proven to me that if I teach everything I know, if I spill over from the fullness that is inside until I am empty, that emptiness will open poignantly, making room for me to learn, to create, to receive.

Frequently when teaching "them that has" in Los Angeles, Pittsburgh, Portland, or Boston, Andy and I hear comments like, "Nothing's really wrong. I'm making more money than I ever have, but my fire has gone out. My dreams are dull." As these people describe their lives, I think of rowing machines, mountain climbing machines, exercise bicycles, cross-country ski machines-so many machines that make us sweat and struggle without taking anybody anyplace.

Andy says, "I've never known a time with so much injury and so much potential sharing the same moment." *Potentia* in Latin means both potency and potentiality. Power and possibility are present as seeds. That possibility and that power both wait to be tapped, like the water table beneath our feet. We don't need to own it, or earn it. We have only to choose how we wish to release and direct it.

Bridges need to be made between "them that knows" and "them that don't." After living the learnings this book offers, you may decide to gather some friends together, and pass on what has been valuable to you. Another bridge. Another chance that these simple skills will pass hand to hand, mouth to ear, imagination to imagination all the way from Damariscotta, Maine to Anacostia, D.C.

> My lifetime listens to yours.
>
> —Muriel Rukeyser

Back to My Roots: The Willow

My father was my grandmother's eighth son, born on the eighth day of the eighth month. There were some other eights involved in his birth, but I don't remember them now. Needless to say, eight was always his lucky number. If you asked him directly if he believed in luck, he'd roll his blue eyes and say it was all superstitious nonsense. Then he'd tell you that hard work and determination were what really mattered to him.

My grandmother told me that I would be a teacher and that I would have a son. She insisted that there was a very important tradition I must remember to follow when he first began to read. I was only nine at the time, so having a son seemed a ridiculous thing to even think about. But traditions I liked. Traditions were candles and feathers and mysterious words and moving hands like flowers in a wind. When she spoke to me about something important, she often placed her warm palm on my forehead, and our minds became like two watercolors bleeding into one another.

"When your son learns to read, the very first time, you must give him some honeycake, something sweet to eat. His mind will tie the two things together from that moment on. Learning and sweetness. Don't forget this!"

I asked her if someone had given her something sweet to eat when she was a young reader. She half-smiled and shook her head. "I never learned to read. We had no books in my village, and besides I was a girl. Girls were for cooking and cleaning, not for books and learning. That's the way it was where I came from in Russia. That's why I wanted to leave. That, and the Cossacks and the *pogroms.*"

I knew she didn't want to talk about the pogroms. Her first two children were killed in a pogrom, and her brother and her mother. I wasn't sure what a pogrom actually was. I just knew it had to do with drunken soldiers and Jewish people being shot for fun late at night, because they were Jewish.

I decided not to ask her any more about the pogroms, but I did want to know if she had given my father honeycake when he had learned to read. Her eyes got all red, as if they were bleeding, and her words got sing-songy, as if she were mourning someone who had

Creative minds have always been known to survive any kind of bad training.

—Anna Freud

died.

"We were too poor then for honey. Your grandfather was working in the sweatshop, and eight children were a lot of mouths to feed. We didn't have money for sweet things, and your father had to drop out of school too soon so he could work and help out. He never learned to read too well. It is the one thing I am ashamed of. That is why it is so important that you teach **your** son and many other people to love learning. Then it will be all right about your father. His root will sprout through you and your son, and it will be all right. You and your son will learn to read for me, for your father, for my sons in the pogrom, for all of us, and it will be all right."

I'm remembering sitting in my father's office in Chicago. It was a very big room with glass windows that looked out over a highway. I went there many days after school. Late, after his secretary had gone for the day. He had a secretary because he had become an executive of a large company—the president, in fact. I knew that was very important because his photograph was in the newspaper, and everyone kept talking about how he had worked his way up the ladder. I didn't quite understand what ladder they were talking about, but he and my mother laughed a lot and had many parties, and my father worked in this big office with all the windows and a tape recorder.

I was ten or eleven, and tape recorders were not tiny Walkman things. They were too heavy to lift, with two big plastic reels filled with thin brown shiny ribbon. Next to this tape recorder were many piles of papers. Business papers, newspapers, many kinds and colors of papers printed, typewritten, or just handwritten.

My father and I shared a secret. No one in his company knew that he couldn't read. He'd hold papers up between his hands, and furrow his eyebrows just a little, shaking his head slowly, mumbling "Hmmm" as his eyes moved randomly across the pages he was turning. He even kept a book on the maple nightstand next to his bed, which he'd open, and hold for a few minutes until he'd fall asleep, his "reading" glasses perched on the end of his nose. I'm not even sure if my mother or sister knew. I guess he figured that if he acted as if he could read, then some magical day he'd be able to.

He certainly did not want the other men in his company to

People who have not been in Narnia sometimes think that a thing cannot be good and terrible at the same time.

—C.S. Lewis

Each of us must make our own true way, and when we do, that way will express the universe.

—Suzuki Roshi

know of this. I was his ally, his accomplice, the guardian of this secret vulnerability. I'd put my school books on the floor, push the button on the tape recorder, and begin to read one of the papers in the stacks on the desk. He'd go to sales meetings, make brilliant oral presentations, give interviews to the newspapers, and I'd just sit at that big mahogany desk in the brown leather swivel chair reading memos, reports, correspondence, and stock quotations.

He always left a quarter tucked under the green leather desk blotter, so I could buy myself a hot fudge sundae on the way home. Something sweet after my reading.

Several years later he and I were walking by the reservoir near our house, when we came upon an immense weeping willow. I ran under it and looked upward. A wind blew the branches back and forth across my face. I laughed so hard he came and stood next to me and did the same thing.

"It's like magic green fingers, Daddy. The tree is talking to us, making friends, loving us with these long green leaf fingers. I wish we had a willow tree like this one, Daddy."

My father was a sucker for a wish. Since I had been little, if I said I wished for something, I knew he'd try to make it come true. He told me that the willow tree had a very strong root, and suggested we take a few branches home with us. We carefully selected two. When we got home, we put them into ginger ale bottles filled with water. Each night when he'd come back from work, we'd go in the garage to check and see if the branches had rooted.

When the bottles were finally filled with wiggly white hairs, we marched into the back yard to plant them. He dug his in first, and then instructed me to let my instinct find the place to put mine. He told me that I'd have to find a place just the right distance from his. Then, when they were fully grown, their branches would touch. He told me that when that happened, I'd know we could never really be separated.

I was afraid I'd do it wrong, it seemed so important. But I closed my eyes, got very still inside like I used to with my grandmother. It was as if I could feel her hand laid on me again, her heart thrumming in my mind. And then I knew! Jumping both feet on the shovel, I began to dig a hole in what I was sure was just the right place.

Several years after my father died, when I was a woman and my son was in college, Andy and I went back to that house on Bon Air Avenue in New Rochelle. I took him for a walk around the reservoir, and we climbed on the cliff in the woods I used to call my "Just For Me Place." I didn't know the current owners of the house, but going inside was not important anyhow. What mattered was those two willow trees in the back yard.

We tiptoed past the curtained windows, past the slate patio where my father used to barbecue hamburgers proudly. I half expected my cocker spaniel, Honey, to come running after us as we walked quietly past the rock garden.

And they were there—two immense willows. Things from childhood always seem smaller when you're grown up, but these willows were even larger than I had imagined them to be. Their yellow-green trunks were big enough around to hug. But even though they were at least 20 or 30 feet apart, their branches did **indeed** touch one another as they danced in the wind.

Andy held me and I began to cry as we stood there. I cried for my father's ancestors who had never known land they could call their own. I cried for his mother who used to carry a handful of earth with her in a small wooden box so she would be able to feel at home in the tenements of New York City. I cried for the man who could not read, but who had managed to live on land he could call his own, land where he could plant weeping willow trees with his daughter so they would never be apart.

We took a thin branch from each of those trees back to Vermont. Mine sprouted, Andy's did not. We dug a deep hole next to the pond, and tended it daily until it too had grown into a tree.

On August 8, 1988, at 8:08 in the evening, just as the sun was beginning to slip into the lake like an orange slice of forever, Andy and I cut eight shoots off the willow. Each one was carefully placed into a ginger ale bottle full of water. Holding each other, we sang "Happy Birthday" as loud as we could.

Most of the shoots did not make it through the winter. We carried one that did in a little white china pot to my mother in Denver,

> Artistic growth is, more than anything else, a refining sense of truthfulness. The stupid believe that to be truthful is easy; only the artist, the great artist, knows how difficult it really is.
>
> —Willa Cather

Colorado. It died several days later. The eighth shoot survived, of course. As I write this, it sits on my desk in a plain red clay pot, next to the piles of paper scribbled with notes, the hundreds of pages typed full of stories for this book.

There is no reason it should have lived indoors. Willows need room and water and rich wet earth. I like to think it brings my father close to me, while I write this book he never would have been able to read. I like to think he prints his shape upon the pages, the way a finger leaves its impression in warm wax.

I like to think my grandmother comes to these pages too, laying her warm palm on my forehead and whispering, "Don't forget to tell them to eat some honeycake after they read this book. The boys and the girls. The men and the women. The Russians and the Americans. Remind them to eat some honeycake so their minds will tie the two things together from that moment on. Learning and sweetness. Remember this now!"

I have a deep intuition of the Possible in you, in me; of the force working within humans that opens our minds and carries us forward. It is my dream that what I have shared will help you find friendship, shelter, and craft. I ask you to take the ideas from this book as seed, as water, as fire; live your life into them, make them real. May they shine brightly and steadily for you, today and always.

Aloneness and connection are like tides in the sea of your heart, separate tides, flowing in and out.

—M.C. Richards,
Centering

Bibliography

Borysenko, Joan. *Guilt Is the Teacher. Love Is the Lesson*. New York: Warner Books, 1990.

Brain/Mind Bulletin. Los Angeles: Interface Press.

Briggs, John. *Fire In the Crucible*. New York: St. Martin's Press, 1988.

Campbell, Don G. *The Roar of Silence: Healing Powers of Breath, Tone and Music*. Wheaton, Ill.: Theosophical Publishers, 1988.

Cappachione, Lucia. *The Power of Your Other Hand*. N. Hollywood, Ca.: Newcastle Publishing Co., 1988.

Carbo, Marie; Dunn, Rita and Kenneth. *Teaching Students to Read Through Their Individual Learning Styles*. Englewood Cliffs, NJ: Prentice Hall, 1986.

Csikszentmihalyi, Mihaly. *Flow: The Psychology Of Optimal Experience*. Harper and Row, 1990.

Dobson, Terry and Miller, Victor. *Giving in to Get Your Way*, New York: Delacorte, 1978.

Edwards, Betty. *Drawing on the Right Side of the Brain*. Los Angeles: J.P. Tarcher, 1989.

Eisler, Riane. *The Chalice and the Blade*. San Francisco: Harper and Row, 1987.

Fisher, Roger and Ury, William. *Getting to Yes*. Boston: Houghton Mifflin, 1981.

Fox, Matthew. *Common Boundary*, July/August 1980.

_____. *Original Blessing*. Santa Fe, NM: Bear and Co. 1983.

Goldberg, Natalie. *Writing Down the Bones*. Boston: Shambhala, 1986.

Goleman, Daniel E. and John, Roy. "How the Brain Works—A New Theory." *Psychology Today*, May 1976.

Hall, Edward T. *Beyond Culture*. Garden City, New York: Anchor Press/Doubleday & Co., 1976.

Hanh, Thich Nhat. *Being Peace*. Berkeley: Parallex Press, 1987.

_____. *The Sun My Heart*. Berkeley: Parallex Press, 1988.

Heckler, Richard Strozzi. *The Anatomy of Change*. Boston: Shambhala, 1984.

Kabbat-Zinn, Jon. *Full Catastrophe Living*. New York: Delacorte Press, 1990.

Klauser, Henriette Ann. *Writing on Both Sides of the Brain*. San Francisco: Harper and Row, 1986.

Kopp, Sheldon. *Raise Your Right Hand Against Fear*. Minneapolis: CompCare Publishers, 1988.

Krishnamurti, J. *The First and Last Freedom*. Wheaton, Ill.: Theosophical Pub. Co., 1968

_____. *Think On These Things*. New York: Harper & Row, 1964.

LeGuin, Ursula. *Dancing At the Edge Of the World*. New York: Grove Press, 1989

Lessing, Doris. *The Golden Notebook*. New York: Simon and Schuster, 1962.

Lewis, C. Day. *The Poetic Image*. London: Oxford University Press, 1948.

Luke, Helen. *The Inner Story*. New York: Crossroad Press, 1982.

Masters, Robert and Houston, Jean. *Mind Games*. New York: Viking, 1972.

Neihardt, John G. *Black Elk Speaks*. Lincoln, NE: University of Nebraska Press, 1961.

Pearce, Joseph Chilton. *The Bond Of Power*. New York: Dutton, 1981.

Reed, William. *Ki: A Practical Guide For Westerners*. New York: Japan Publications, 1986.

Richards, M.C. *Centering*. Middletown, Ct: Wesleyan University Press, 1989.

_____. *Towards Wholeness*. Ct: Wesleyan University Press, 1980

Rossi, Ernest and Cheek, David B. *Mind Body Therapy*. New York: Norton & Co, 1988.

Safransky, Sy. "The Man in the Mirror." *The Sun*, December 1989.

Satir, Virginia. *Peoplemaking*. Palo Alto, Ca.: Science and   Behavior, 1972.

shange, ntozake. "Conversations With the Ancestors" *Riding the Moon In Texas*. New York: St. Martin's Press, 1987.

Stafford, William. *You Must Revise Your Life*. Ann Arbor: The University Of Michigan Press, 1986.

Tohei, Koichi. *Ki In Daily Life*, New York: Japan Publications, 1978.

Williams, Linda V. *Teaching for the Two Sided Mind*. New York: Simon & Schuster, 1983.

Wise, Anna. *The High Performance Mind*. New York: Tarcher, 1995.

List of Charts

States of Consciousness, 22
Symbolic Languages of Thinking, 37
Triggers to States of Consciousness, 59
The Six Patterns: A Mental Topography, 74-75
Examples of Percepual Language—Analogies, 153

The ancient redwood trees of Northern California, huge as they are, have a very shallow root system, yet they cannot be blown over by the strongest wind. The secret of their stability is the interweaving of each tree_s roots with those that stand by it. Thus, a vast network of support is formed just beneath the surface. In the wildest of storms, these trees hold each other up.

Acknowledgments

Bowing to My Support

Edith & William Mechanic
Andy Bryner
David Peck
Mary Jane Ryan
Anne Powell

Joanne Whelden, Maria Chiriboga, Lisa Caine, Peris Gumz,
Larry Rippel, Rachel Edwards, Peggy Tileston, Mary Pat Mengato,
Dale and Tom Lowery, June LaPointe, Shauna Frazier, Jane LaPointe, Marjean Bailey,
Tami Simon, Judy Brown, Rita Cleary
The Madison Study Group, The Pennsylvania Study Group,
The East Coast Study Group, The California Study Group

Will Glennon
Ame Beanland
Emily Miles
Brenda Knight
Jennifer Brontsema

Thich Nhat Hanh, Milton Erickson, Richard Kuboyama,
Terry Dobson, Lloyd Miyashiro

Index

A

Affirmation, 178
Alcohol
　effect on perceptual pattern, 173
Art
　of communicating, 189
Auditory Channel (see also Perceptual
　Channels), 34, 127

B

Bailey, Rev. Marjean, 191
"Bedroom Bodies,"155
"Bedroom Ears,"154
"Bedroom Eyes,"155
Beginner's mind, 10-12
Boundary setting, 31
Brain waves, 21
　Alpha, 26, 30, 34, 54, 140, 176
　Beta,　23, 30, 34, 38, 43, 54, 140, 148–149,
　　152, 170
　Theta, 28–29, 46, 54, 67, 140, 145, 170,
　　176
　Delta, 45
Bryner, Andy, 118–120, 166–168, 193, 197

C

Carbo, Marie & Dunn, Kenneth, 5
Categorization
　dangers of, 188
Centers of gravity, 188
Centering, 188
Channels (see Perceptual Channels)
"Clean hands,"188–190
Cocaine
　effect on perceptual patterns, 173, 176
Combinations
　effect on perceptual patterns, 156, 160
Communication

bridging gaps, 142,150
improving, 147, 149, 154, 165, 179
in intimate relationships, 184
with children, 150, 160–163, 182
with compassion, 8, 141, 188
with different perceptual languages, 142,
　148, 177, 185
Compassion, 66
Composite Portraits,
　AKV, 87
　AVK, 81
　KAV, 118
　KVA, 110
　VAK, 94
　VKA, 102
Conflict
　resolution, 168
Conscious Mind, Mode (see also Organizing
　Mind, Mode), 23–24, 125, 148, 163, 172,
　178
Context
　changing, 53
Creative Mode (see also Unconscious mode),
　31, 52
Curiosity, 9, 60, 131, 144, 146, 153

D

"Deep Reflection," 124
Dialogue
　with frequently asked questions, 170–186
Drugs
　effects on perceptual patterns, 173–176

E

Edison, Thomas, 31
Education, 13
Edwards, Rachel, 172
EEG, 20

Empathy, 137, 139, 181
Empirical learning, 10
Erickson, Milton, 4, 23, 135
Ethics
   use of approach, 8, 188
Expressing (see also Communicating), 38
Eye contact, 44, 49, 65, 69, 75, 81, 87, 93,
   100, 103, 109, 117, 171
"Eye shy,"46, 69, 89

F
"Feelages,"34
Filtering, 154, 180
"Flat affect," 42

G
Groups
   speaking to, 68–69, 137

H
Hall, Edward, 5–6
Haydn, 145
Hypnotherapy, 4, 26, 34

I
Ignorance
   invincible, 192
   vincible, 192
Intelligences, 61
   natural, 3, 5, 8, 16–17
Intimacy, 2, 65, 176, 183–184
   avoidance, 183
Intuition, 10, 28, 52

K
Ki-Aikido, 9, 188
Kindred Clubs, 41
   creating auditorily, 48
   creating kinesthetically, 50
   creating visually, 49
   organizing auditorily, 41
   organizing kinesthetically, 42

   organizing visually, 43
   sorting auditorily, 57
   sorting kinesthetically, 57
   sorting visually, 56
Kinesthetic Channel (see also Perceptual
   Channel), 34
Kuboyama, Richard, 9, 188

L
Landowska, Wanda, 11
Learning
   and sweetness, 194, 198
   safely, 10
   styles, 45
Left-brain, 2, 26, 45, 176

M
Marijuana
   effect on perceptual patterns, 139, 173
Martial arts, 4, 26, 143
Matching Perceptual Patterns, 156–157
Meditation, 188
Mental
   metabolism, 20
   syntax, 3
Mengato, Mary Pat, 172
Metaphoric Learning, 8, 125
Metaphors, 69, 92, 96
Middle Third, 54, 60
Mind
   balancing, 143
   beginners, 10–12
   conscious (see organizational mode)
   of heart, 2
   powerful, 135
   subconscious (see sorting mode)
   unconscious (see creative mode)
Mother Theresa, 31
Movement
   compared in different patterns, 172–173

N

Natural intelligence, 3, 5, 8, 16–17, 67
Non-dominant hand, 53, 177

O

"Odd ones," 5, 7
One Point (see also centering), 188
"One-way mind," 23
Operator's Manual for getting along with...
    AKVs, 88
    AVKs, 82
    KAVs, 120
    KVAs, 111
    VAKs, 95
    VKAs, 103
Organization
    of book, 8, 45
Organizational Mind, Mode (see Conscious
    Mind, Mode)
"Over-analyzing," 130, 132

P

"Paper Conversation," 95
Parentheses
    of perceptual combinations, 156, 166
Pattern Snapshot
    AKV, 86
    AVK, 80
    KAV, 116
    KVA, 108
    VAK, 92
    VKA, 100
Perceptual Fluency, 151, 153
Perceptual Languages, 35, 50, 148, 161
    communicating with different, 142, 148
    shifting, 124
Perceptual Patterns, 66–67, 71, 170
    assessing, 67
    combinations, 156, 160
    effect of drugs, 173–176
    parentheses, 156, 166
    match, 156–157

single point, 156, 163
scramble, 156, 163
specific
    AKV, 62–63, 65–73, 75, 85–89, 145, 155,
        163, 170–186
    AVK, 62, 69–73, 76, 79–83, 126, 128, 147,
        155, 170–186
    KAV, 63, 69–73, 76, 115–121, 137, 147,
        155, 163, 166, 170–186
    KVA, 63, 65, 69–73, 76, 107–113, 135,
        147, 154, 160, 170–186
    VAK, 63, 65, 67, 69–73, 75, 91–97, 129,
        155, 157, 160, 170–186
    VKA, 63, 67, 69–73, 76, 99–105, 132, 145,
        154, 170–186
Personal Thinking Patterns, 8, 16, 77
Personality, 64
Physically challenged, 170
"Pinwheel Talking," 47, 181
Potentia, 193
Practices, 9–10
    Awkward and Alive, 150
    Building a Bridge of Communication, 147
    Centering: Finding Yourself with Another, 143
    Creative Approach to Problem Solving, 53
    Discovering Your Pattern from Inside Out, 67
    Getting to the Point, 40
    Honoring Wisdom, Finding Intent, 12
    Move over Ann Landers, 71
    Noticing How Life Affects You, 58
    Noticing Peoples' Perceptual Differences, 44
    Overlapping, 150
    Rafting the River of Your Mind, 124
    Ways of Knowing: Conscious, 23
    Ways of Knowing: Subconscious, 25
    Ways of Knowing: Unconscious, 28

R

Rapport, 55, 149
Recharging, 180
Respect, 168
Responsibility, 192
Right-brain, 26, 28

Rippel, Larry, 172

S

Safe learning, 10
"Scatterbrain," 185
Schweitzer, Albert, 31
Scramble
    in perceptual combination, 156, 160
Single Point
    in perceptual combination, 156, 163
Sister Agnes, 192
"Sizzle Point," 143, 168
Sorting Mind, Mode (see Subconscious Mind,
    Mode)
Speaking
    casually, 169
    to groups, 69–70, 137
Spiral of Thinking, 21–22, 45, 151
Spiritual connection, 29
States of Consciousness, 8, 21, 36
States of Mind (see States of Consciousness)
Stories, 8
    Are We Making Love or Having a Fight?, 157
    Caught in the Middle, 160
    Coming out of the Closet, 163
    The Doodle Bug, 51
    From Carousel to Compass, 132
    From Vesuvius to Stradivarius, 128
    Giving without Giving Herself away, 137
    Meeting in a Closet, 166
    Paralysis by Analysis, 139
    Tame it and Aim it, 125
    Untying the Knots, 135
    The Willow, 194
Subconscious Mind, Mode, 25, 27, 53, 125,
    148, 178
Symbolic Languages (see also Perceptual
    Languages), 8, 38,
    40, 45, 53, 64, 151–152

T

"Talkstory," 125–126
Thich Nhat Hanh, 191

Tileston, Peggy, 163
Threshold, 39
    of concentration, 46–47, 62
Trance (see Hypnotherapy)
Transconscious, 28
Triggers
    to states of consciousness, 34, 36, 40, 45, 58,
    183

U

Unconscious Mind, Mode (see also Creative
    Mind, Mode), 28, 30, 46, 52, 125, 127,
    148, 154, 178

V

Vermont Training Group, 51
Visual Channel (see also Perceptual Channels),
    34, 55
"Virtuous Intent," 143
Visualization, 49, 180
Vocational Training Program, 163

W

West Coast Study Group, 137
Writing
    with dominant hand, 177
    with non-dominant hand, 53, 177

If you found **The Open Mind** useful, chances are you will enjoy
Dr. Dawna Markova's other books:

No Enemies Within: *A Creative Process for Discovering What's Right about What's Wrong*

How Your Child Is Smart: *A Life-Changing Approach to Learning*

An Unused Intelligence: *Physical Thinking for 21st Century Leadership*

Look for these titles in your favorite bookstore or contact Conari Press at:

CONARI PRESS
2550 Ninth Street, Suite 101
Berkeley, CA 94710
phone: 800-685-9595
fax: 510-649-7190
e-mail: conaripub@aol.com

The Open Mind is also available in audio as a 6-cassette learning course
based on the book. (8 hours, $59.95, ISBN 1-56455-349-3)
Available from Sounds True Audio. For information or to order, call: 800-333-9185